YOU THE HEALER

THE WORLD-FAMOUS SILVA METHOD ON HOW TO HEAL YOURSELF AND OTHERS

José Silva
Robert B. Stone

YOU THE HEALER

THE WORLD-FAMOUS SILVA METHOD ON HOW TO HEAL YOURSELF AND OTHERS

José Silva
Robert B. Stone

EBD
Embassy Books
www.embassybooks.in

YOU THE HEALER - The World-Famous Silva Method on How to Heal Yourself and Others By José Silva and Robert B. Stone

Original English language publication 1989 by H J Kramer in a joint venture with
New World Library, California, USA.

First Edition 2024

Published in India by:

Embassy Book Distributors 120, Great Western Building, Maharashtra Chamber of Commerce Lane, Fort, Mumbai 400023
Tel: (91-22) 26689026/26689290
Email: info@embassybooks.in
Website: www.embassybooks.in

Distribution Centres:

Mumbai, Ahmedabad, Bangalore, Kolkata, Chennai, Hyderabad, New Delhi, Pune

ISBN: 978-81-19726-78-3

Cover Design by: Sonal Churi

Printed and bound in India by Repro India Ltd., India

To
my wife, Paula,
my sister, Josefina,
my brother, Juan,
and all my sons and daughters:
José Silva, Jr.,
Isabel Silva de las Fuentes,
Ricardo Silva,
Margarita Silva Cantu,
Antonio Silva,
Ana Maria Silva Martínez,
Hilda Silva González,
Laura Silva,
Delia Silva Pérez,
Diana Silva.

José Silva

To Our Readers

The books we publish are our contribution to an emerging world based on cooperation rather than on competition, on affirmation of the human spirit rather than on self-doubt, and on the certainty that all humanity is connected. Our goal is to touch as many lives as possible with a message of hope for a better world.

Hal and Linda Kramer, Publishers

Preface

You need not live a life of sickness.

You need not die from ill health.

It is your natural state to be healthy.

It is your right to live a perfectly healthy life right up to the day you die of natural causes.

In this exciting breakthrough book, José Silva reveals what he has learned from his pathfinding research, begun in 1944, into the psychosomatic causes and cures of illness.

You will read many case histories here of people who had suffered for years but were able to heal themselves in a very short time when they learned to apply the tremendous power of their minds.

You will learn about actual experiences with first-aid procedures that have quickly corrected injuries sustained in accidents.

Most importantly, you will learn how to prevent disease, and even accidents, from entering your life, so that you can live a healthy, safe, happy existence and help your loved ones do the same.

Is all this really possible?

Since 1966, millions of people in seventy-two countries have learned and applied the unique Silva Method of Mind Development and Stress Control to their lives, and over and over they say, "Thank you for showing me how to improve my life."

This book will change your life when you read it and follow its easy step-by-step instructions. Your miraculous results will quickly convince you of the program's effectiveness, and you will wonder why everyone is not using it.

That day will come!

Today is the day for you to begin to use these techniques so you and your loved ones can live happily and healthily every minute for the rest of your lives.

About the Authors

José Silva is a self-educated lay research scientist whose explorations into the healing arts have never been limited by the conventional practices of scientific research. His probing into the curiosities of our world led him to discover truths that are finally, today, being confirmed by conventional laboratory research. This book represents the findings of his research in the field of healing and the maintenance of superior health.

Robert B. Stone, Ph.D., is the author and coauthor of more than seventy self-help books. He is a Silva Method lecturer, has circled the globe twice speaking on the powers of the mind, and has launched Silva Mind Control in Japan, New Zealand, and Thailand. He is a member of the New York Academy of Science and MENSA.

Contents

Introduction

A man sits in a comfortable chair, closes his eyes, and takes three deep breaths. The observer does not know that on the first exhalation the man has pictured the number three three times; on the second exhalation, the number two three times; and on the third exhalation, the number one three times. Nor does the observer know that this man has also counted backward from ten to one and has then visualized a profoundly curative scene.

An observer who could peek inside this man's mind would see that the man is picturing himself rubbing an imaginary salve on his right arm in the area of the elbow, where he has been experiencing pain. He is picturing his arm perfect. In a few seconds the man will have ended his mental work and opened his eyes. In a few hours he will be on the tennis court in an energetic singles game with no "back talk" from the elbow.

This man is a Silva Method graduate. He has been trained to enter a level of consciousness where he can control his mind to affect his body.

N.L. had arthritis in his finger joints, which was interfering with his job as an architectural draftsman. Periodically, he relaxed and visualized the lumps on his fingers. He then pictured himself vacuuming his fingers. He pictured the arthritis as a powder being sucked up by the vacuum cleaner. Then he imagined his fingers free of lumps and saw himself working again at his job painlessly.

N.L. did this each day, spending three minutes visualizing the problem being corrected and himself in perfect health.

Within a week, his daily three-minute investment began to pay off: the swelling and lumps on his fingers were materially reduced. Within three weeks he was free of the arthritis problem.

R.S. had chest pains. His doctor diagnosed them as angina pectoris. He explained that this was the result of hardening of the arteries. A crust called plaque was forming in his arteries, and those that fed blood to his heart were partially blocked. The doctor recommended a low-cholesterol, low-fat, high-fiber diet and a program of mild exercise, such as walking and swimming. R.S. followed the instructions for diet and exercise but added one more step: programming. He relaxed and visualized the partially blocked arteries to his heart. He then imagined that he was rooting them out with a pipe cleaner. His final mental picture was one of these arteries free of plaque. He did these visualizations daily, and within one month the chest pains had become noticeably less frequent. Within two months the chest pains had disappeared completely and years later had still not returned.

For much of her adult life, M.W. had regularly experienced severe menstrual distress. She began a program of "talking" to her body and picturing herself without menstrual pain for two minutes a day beginning one week prior to the expected start of her period. When her period arrived following these sessions, she estimated that her usual pain was reduced by 50 percent. Through practice, she has reduced it even further.

There Is a Way

If you had a way of using your mind to get rid of aches and pains, would you do so?

If you had a way of using your mind to fall asleep, would you pass up sleeping pills?

If you had a way to help yourself and your friends to overcome most of your nagging health problems, would you use it?

At long last, even the medical profession is beginning to see how the mind is involved in making us sick and how the mind can be trained to reverse that process and make us well. The Silva Method has been utilizing this insight successfully for decades.

Carl Simonton, M.D., an oncologist at Travis Air Force Base

in California, adapted part of the Silva Method in treating his cancer patients and thereby increased the number of remissions markedly. Dr. Simonton took the Silva Method course under the name of Mind Dynamics. Later, he took advanced work in the Silva Method. He now calls his method the Simonton Method. Independently, Dean Ornish, M.D., while a Clinical Fellow in Medicine at Harvard Medical School, devised relaxation and visualization methods for heart patients and, by combining them with diet and exercise, successfully tested them in a controlled scientific study. He found that most of the participants reported a marked reduction in chest pain caused by heart disease and that many became virtually pain free.

It is increasingly common for health practitioners who work with the terminally ill to make use of relaxation and mental imagery because of their positive effects. In 1983, a cover story in *Time* magazine referring to the Simonton Method quoted Boston University psychiatrist Sanford Cohen: "Bizarre as it seems, the technique has helped 'significant numbers of terminal patients survive beyond all expectations.'" Since Dr. Simonton's exposure to the Silva Method, and his integration of it into his world-famous training program, hundreds of physicians and thousands of nurses have taken the training.

In 1973, astronaut Edgar Mitchell founded the Institute of Noetic Sciences, devoted to "broadening knowledge of the nature and potentials of mind and consciousness and to applying that knowledge to the enhancement of human well-being and the quality of life on the planet."

Previously, support for Simonton was generally assumed to come solely from off-beat, even odd sources. Now, the Noetics Institute reports that the following formerly "far-out" concepts are commonly accepted in mainstream medical circles:

1. An individual is inherently capable of controlling his or her own physiological processes to a greater degree than ever before thought possible.

2. Healing always involves both mind and body as well as what many call the spirit.
3. Negative emotions can have adverse psychophysiological effects.
4. Positive emotions can have positive psychophysiological effects.
5. The mind has many avenues of contact with bodily processes, some of which can "tip the scales" toward healing.

This change in climate has occurred since I first "went public" with the Silva Method in the late 1960s, and it is cause for rejoicing. The strict allopathic approach characteristic of medical treatment until then has given way to acceptance that mental imagery can attain real and useful results.

Athletes are now training themselves for greater skill and endurance by picturing themselves playing the perfect game, running the perfect race. When amateurs tee up on the golf course and take furtive looks at the water hazard to the left, then at the wooded rough to the right, they are programming themselves for a poorly aimed drive. Professionals, by seeing only the flag at the hole, program themselves for the straight drive.

Pictures we hold in our minds have demonstrable effects on our bodies. Positive pictures produce desirable effects. Negative pictures produce undesirable effects.

That the mind can make us sick and that it also can make us well is one of the most important discoveries of the twentieth century.

More and more people are beginning to understand that when you change your mental climate, your body follows suit. If you know how, you can use your mind to keep yourself looking radiantly healthy, your immune system working efficiently, and your energy levels high.

You can use your mind to quickly get rid of pesky health problems such as colds, headaches, and chronic aches and pains. If you know how, you can even use it to help your health-care specialist rid you of such serious ailments as cancer.

And you can use your mind to help others enjoy these same benefits—at a distance and without their even knowing about it.

Sounds incredible? These are scientific facts! Science now acknowledges that your mind can project through fields of intelligence and affect matter. Recently, at a Texas laboratory, subjects were able to intentionally increase or decrease the electrical activity of the skin of other people twenty meters away in another room. And these weren't experts, either—just ordinary people from different walks of life.

In another laboratory—the Backster Foundation in San Diego, California—researchers were able to demonstrate (in the presence of author Robert Stone) that human thought can affect human body cells across a room.

Such experiments demonstrate that you and your friends can live longer, happier, healthier lives if you know how to control your own minds.

This book teaches you to do just that. Millions of Silva Method graduates in more than seventy countries are able to use their minds not only for maintaining better health but for controlling intuition, increasing creativity, raising I.Q. levels, and enhancing problem-solving ability. In this book you will learn all you need to know to use this method for getting well, staying well, and helping your family and friends to do the same.

Your Mental Computer Runs Your Body

The Silva Method shows you how to harness the cybernetic, or computerlike, powers of your brain to gain greater health and enhanced mental functioning. After reading this book, you will know how to keep your mind from making you sick. You will know how to insulate yourself from stress. You will know how to correct health problems and how to help your doctor to help you.

We learn how to get sick at a very young age. We are actually programmed for it with such messages as, "If you get your feet wet, you'll catch cold." The brain neurons accept such programming as instruction, an order to be obeyed. And so such a message becomes a self-fulfilling prophecy.

We watch others get sick. We picture it happening to us. That's called worry. Worry, too, is programming. The pictures we hold in our minds also act as orders to be obeyed. Our thoughts and words become programming. Negative thoughts and expressions of feeling become negative or unwanted programming. Positive thoughts and expressions of feeling become positive or wanted programming. Negative programming produces unhappiness, failure, and ill health. Positive programming spells happiness, success, and good health.

If you are programmed to think negatively, you are trapped in a negative pattern. If you don't change your programming, you will remain the same. That is why people who want to be healthy are still filling our hospitals. They need to reprogram themselves.

Overcoming your programming is an uphill battle. You can change temporarily, but, unless you alter the program, eventually you must revert to your programmed behavior. It takes reprogramming to change. For example, you can change your programmed eating habits by going on some new regimen. We call that "going on a diet." But few people can stay on a diet permanently. When they go off their diet and back to their former programmed ways of eating, they usually gain back all the weight they lost on the diets. They need to reprogram their eating habits. Negative programming that produces illness can be stopped dead in its tracks with new, positive programming.

The Silva Method Formula-Type Techniques

Reprogramming yourself for better health with the Silva Method is done through mental imagery at a mental state or consciousness level called the alpha level.

Alpha is a level at which brain waves slow to about half their normal frequency during wakefulness. We put out fourteen to twenty-one brain-energy pulsations per second when we are actively awake. Researchers call that normal wakefulness the beta level. When you go to bed at night and fall asleep, these brain pulsations slow down.

An electroencephalograph, a machine that measures these pulsations, would show that as you relaxed in bed with your eyes closed, your brain pulsations were decreasing by half. Seven to fourteen pulsations per second has been designated by the researchers to be the alpha level, a relaxed level of sleepy wakefulness. As you enter sleep, your brain waves slow even more. Light sleep, between four and seven pulsations per second, is called theta level. Deepest sleep, anything below four pulsations per second, is called delta level.

Figure 1 illustrates these four levels. Note that deep alpha is called the basic plane. This is the lowest frequency of alpha used in most Silva techniques. It is this natural, comfortable, peaceful, relaxed state that we pass through on our way to sleep at night and on awakening in the morning. In this book, you will learn to stay in this level and use it to heal yourself and others and reprogram yourself.

What has the alpha level to do with the health benefits described here? Researchers working with biofeedback equipment have come to realize that good things are happening to the body when the brain is at the alpha level. Stressed organs and systems are recuperating and becoming revitalized. Blood pressure is becoming normalized. Pulse rate is stabilizing. In Laredo, Texas, while researching how to put more of our minds to work for us, researchers found that at the alpha level subjects gained control of formerly uncontrollable functions. Faculties considered to be subconscious or unconscious became more conscious. Habits came under more conscious control. Automatic bodily functions also became more controllable. Geniuslike faculties of the human mind that only occasionally give us flashes of insight can now be triggered on command at the alpha level to solve problems as in kind of a supermind.

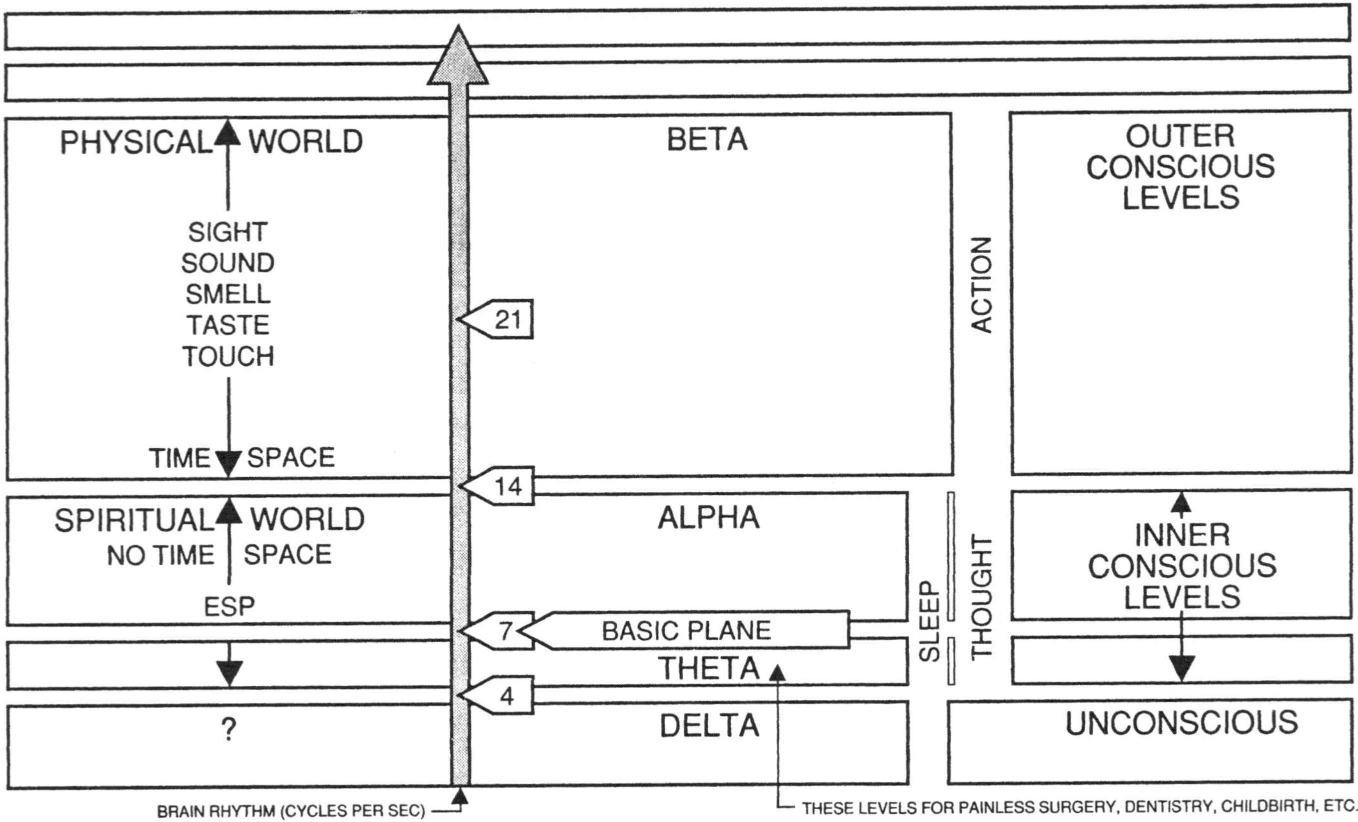

SCALE OF BRAIN EVOLUTION

Figure 1. The Four Levels of Brain Activity

An Overview of the Silva Training

You have already programmed your brain to take over much of your life. You get up in the morning, put on your clothes, tie your shoes, brush your teeth, drive your car—all without giving these activities a second thought. With the Silva Method you will learn to use your mind to gain more conscious control of your life. You will learn ways to use your mind to

- fall asleep at will;
- wake up any time without an alarm clock;
- stay awake when drowsy;
- get rid of a headache;
- solve problems by means of a dream;
- stop smoking;
- lose weight;
- remember long lists easily;
- study with greater concentration and recall;
- answer difficult problems;
- reach goals;
- get rid of pain anywhere in your body;
- correct abnormalities in your body;
- trigger both brain hemispheres to work for you;
- become more creative and perceptive;
- correct health problems in others.

You will acquire these sixteen benefits through what I call formula-type techniques. By *formula* I mean "First do this, then do this, then do this"—simple mental steps, performed mostly at the alpha level.

More than eight million graduates in some seventy countries have taken a minimum of thirty-two hours of instruction in the Silva Method. The course takes its participants through ten hours of controlled relaxation to correct such problems as fatigue, insomnia, tension-type headaches, and migraine headaches. It is during this initial segment of the training that participants learn to go to the alpha level quickly and easily and to use that alpha level both to control the body's vitality and energy and to solve problems without strain or stress.

In the succeeding segment of the training, participants learn greater control of psychological and physiological functions traditionally considered to be subconscious and not consciously controllable. They learn keys to improving memory and concentration, first aid for eliminating chronic or sudden pain, means of controlling or eliminating unwanted habits, and ways of using more of the mind for problem solving.

In the third and fourth segments of the training, a sequence of imagining exercises set up points of reference that enable trainees to control subjective functioning. The left hemisphere of the brain is oriented to the physical world, while the right hemisphere is oriented to the nonphysical—or, you might say, the spiritual—realm, which is creative. In effect, the new reference points imbue the right hemisphere of the brain with the benefits of the left hemisphere, allowing it to function under conscious control for increased awareness, enhanced creativity, and control of health. This phase of the training enables graduates to visualize their bodies, imagine corrections taking place, and then experience the improvement. In the final hours of the training, participants get unquestionable verification of their ability to "sense" other people unknown to them, identify their health problems, and make corrections.

How to Use This Book

To acquire from a book the benefits available through the thirty-two-hour training sessions, you will need to devote more than thirty-two hours to the effort. The extra time will go toward reading about the steps as well as practicing them.

If you faithfully follow the instructions in Part One, most of the health advantages of the live training can be yours. You can begin to acquire these advantages by tomorrow morning, and they can be well under your control within six weeks.

To achieve these benefits, you will need to practice for a few minutes every morning when you awaken. This is a time when you will already be relaxed and when the practice will yield the best results. Through this practice you will be training yourself to relax even further and thus attain the alpha level. Relaxation itself is therapeutic, and from the moment you begin the practice of relaxation, your body will thrive on it.

Later, as you come to relax more quickly and deeply, you will be able to use the alpha state to program your brain, just as you would a computer, to change unwanted physical symptoms and to correct any troublesome physical conditions.

Read the book entirely through to the end if you wish, but then go back and do the forty sessions, one each day for forty days. At the end of this period, you will be able to perform deep healing work on yourself and others.

Training in the class goes somewhat faster than self-training with the book, because a skilled person is present to help you relax and to read aloud long passages that lead you through the step-by-step procedures that help you achieve deep relaxation. In using the book, you must open your eyes to read these passages, thus interfering with your relaxation. Nevertheless, you will be able to train yourself in forty morning sessions to achieve the requisite relaxation depth. Then you can begin the positive programming that will help eliminate illness.

Part One
The Forty Daily Sessions

Session 1
Relaxation, the Key

In April 1975, M.B., age thirty-four, found himself in a Philadelphia hospital being prepared for surgery. His doctors had discovered that a spinal cord tumor in his neck was causing the progressive paralysis he had been experiencing in his arms and legs for the preceding two months. When the operation was over, the doctors gave him the bad news. They had not been able to remove the tumor because of its involvement with the spinal cord. It was malignant. He had but a year or two to live.

One year later, on the first anniversary of the operation, M.B. was due for an examination. The doctor found nothing. There was no evidence of a tumor. The same doctor who had told M.B. a year ago that he was terminally ill was now saying that he, the physician, must have made a mistake.

What had M.B. done in the interim? He had used the Silva Method.

It was about ten months after the operation that M.B. heard about the Silva Method and took the training. He had practiced what he learned there for only two months prior to his anniversary examination.

For about fifteen minutes, three times a day—upon arising, after lunch, and before retiring—M.B. relaxed deeply. He used a progressive relaxation technique, relaxing first his head, next his neck, then his shoulders, and in progression all of the rest of his body all the way down to his toes. Once relaxed, he pictured his body and the tumor. He imagined the tumor getting smaller. During each of these relaxation sessions he pictured the tumor a bit smaller than the last time. He also imagined that he could see his immune system—the white blood system—going after, dispersing, and eliminating the cancer cells. He told himself that these cancer cells were being passed out of his body every time he went to the bathroom. M.B. also gave himself positive instructions, repeating over and over in this relaxed, meditative state, "Every day, in every way, I'm getting better, better, and better."

When M.B. began to tell his doctor about these mental exercises, his doctor walked out of the room. The process was completely foreign to him. Physicians are rarely able to accept our ability to direct our minds to correct our bodies. These interactions are not taught in medical school—not yet.

It is in order to protect Silva graduates from being embarrassed by skeptics in their home towns that initials are used in many of the examples of healing cited in this book. Still, we occasionally receive a written report from a graduate who is so eager to share his or her success with others that permission is granted to use the full name. In many cases, these reports are even witnessed and notarized. Where that is the case, I have happily included the names in the case descriptions.

Activating More of Your Mind

By now, you have realized that the key to the Silva Method is relaxation. But the relaxation taught here is not passive. You will learn to relax actively. Both achieving and using this state of relaxation is an active process. By using our minds to relax and then to picture positive images, we are activating the creative role of our brain—a function of the right hemisphere that is seldom fully involved in our thinking.

Simply stated, the Silva Method places us in conscious control of deep levels of our mind. It enables us to employ relatively slow brain waves (alpha) to expand our awareness and our problem-solving abilities. Health problems are the easiest to solve, because we are in control of the very source of these problems.

Programming Our Behavior With Words and Pictures

Our bodies are equipped for self-healing. We interfere with this natural process by reacting to events with worry and stress. We can withdraw this interference by responding to external events with relaxed reactions.

We can also harness a healing energy by conceiving positive mental pictures and positive mentally verbalized instructions.

The Silva Method for better health is based on the use of positive mental instructions during relaxation. The method is simple and easy and becomes more effective with practice. Even though you are a beginner, expect a miracle. Your belief and expectations are a "green light" that tells your brain neurons to change your body's condition for the better.

The moment of decision has come. Do you want to gain more control over your life? If your answer is yes, you will profit not only with respect to your health but also in regard to every other facet of your life, as brain neurons that have either been loafing on the job or working against you are suddenly made to work for your betterment.

Because you cannot read this book and relax simultaneously, use this strategy. Read the instructions first; then put the book down, close your eyes, and follow the instructions. Here is your first set of instructions:

1. Sit comfortably in a chair and close your eyes.
2. Take a deep breath, and as you exhale, relax your body.
3. Count slowly backward from 100 to 1.
4. Daydream about some peaceful place you know.
5. Say to yourself mentally, "I will always maintain a perfectly healthy body and mind."
6. Tell yourself mentally that when you open your eyes at the count of 5, you will feel wide awake and better than before. When you reach the count of 3, repeat this. When you open your eyes affirm it again ("I am wide awake and feeling better than before").

Read the instructions once more. Now put the book down and follow them.

You have just experienced *programming*.

Your ability to program will get better with practice. You will gradually relax more quickly and deeply. You will visualize more realistically and your expectation and belief will heighten, thus creating bigger and better results.

I will take you every step of the way. As you approach the end of this book, you will be able to help yourself to good health and use your mind's energy to program others at a distance for better health.

Session 2
Controlling Your Body by Controlling Your Mind

1. Sit comfortably in a chair and close your eyes.
2. Take a deep breath and, as you exhale, relax your body.
3. Count slowly backward from 100 to 1.
4. Daydream about some peaceful place you know.
5. Say to yourself mentally, "I will always maintain a perfectly healthy body and mind."
6. Tell yourself mentally that when you open your eyes at the count of 5, you will feel wide awake and better than before. When you reach the count of 3, repeat this. When you open your eyes, affirm it again ("I am wide awake and feeling better than before").

To be in control of your body, you must control your mind. To learn to control your mind, you must control the alpha level. To control the alpha level, you must control your state of relaxation.

The starting point is to control relaxation. Let me share a story with you from M.R., a lieutenant in the U.S. Navy:

Recently, my eight-year aviation career in the navy was in serious jeopardy. I suffered an allergic reaction to a medication, which caused a brief episode of heart arrhythmia.

An examination at Brooke Army Medical Center revealed that I had a prolapse of the heart mitral valve. This is a congenital defect that can only be diagnosed with sophisticated equipment. Navy regulations prohibit anyone with this defect from being on flight status. Two second opinions confirmed the diagnosis. My case looked open and shut. I was to be examined in three weeks by navy doctors at the Naval Aerospace Institute.

I had not been very consistent in practicing my Silva techniques, but I did remember that abnormalities could be corrected. I came to the alpha level frequently and envisioned a perfect heart with no defects. I also said to myself over and over that my heart was now perfect. This thought ran through my mind day and night until I believed it was so.

Three weeks later I was examined by three navy doctors. No mitral valve prolapse! A congenital defect of thirty-three years had disappeared. All the diagnostic equipment and tests revealed a perfect heart. I was returned to flight status.

I am now a firm believer in the power we have within ourselves to improve our lives.

M.R. relaxed and pictured his heart as perfect. What the mind pictures, the mind creates—if. . . .

This is a big *if*. The mind creates what it pictures *if* it is at the alpha frequency. The brain is a three-pound organ confined to the skull. The mind, limitless in its scope, still depends on the brain. It is at the alpha level that the brain—especially the right hemisphere, the realm of thought, feeling, and emotion—works for us. M.R. pictured his healthy heart and talked to himself when his brain was at this frequency. Mental pictures and verbal instructions are the mechanisms for making physical changes at the subjective, or alpha, level. Using these mechanisms is what we call programming. M.R., while at the alpha level, pictured his heart as perfect, and in this way programmed his mental computer to make it perfect. The mind runs the brain and the brain runs the body. And so the body complied.

Alpha is the key. It takes you away from the objective realm, the physical world, and into the subjective world, the causative or creative realm, the realm that is the *source* of the physical world. Existing on this level gives you a blissful feeling of being alone within yourself. You are aware of the goings-on of the outside world but not actively in it. You are physically and mentally at ease.

"Feeling" the Alpha Level

With each day of practice, you go deeper in the direction of alpha. After you reach alpha, each day of practice brings you into deeper alpha, keeps you from going too deep (back to sleep), and enables you to use your mind for super health—for yourself and for others—while you remain at alpha.

Noted biofeedback researcher Barbara Brown has been able to train people to control their alpha levels by associating the alpha with pleasant feelings.

The coauthor of this book, a Silva lecturer in Hawaii, uses the Hawaiian word *aloha* to mean alpha. *Aloha* means oneness, symbolized by *o*, the middle letter of the word, he explains. Get a handle on oneness and you have reached alpha. He demonstrates at the chalkboard by putting a handle on the *o* in aloha, which changes the *o* to *p*—and the word *aloha* into *alpha*.

Alpha is indeed a delightful feeling. Perhaps the reason is that by entering it we move away from the physical world toward the world within—one step closer to heaven.

When you reach alpha, no bells will ring, no sirens will sound, no voice will announce, "This is alpha."

You will just feel good.

A Positive Attitude

In essence, the Silva Method trains one's awareness at low brain frequencies for specific benefits. This control over the awareness enables the practitioner to improve his or her productivity, and problem-solving ability.

But suppose that during this training you took the attitude that while the method might work for somebody else it would never work for you? This attitude also constitutes programming. To hold it would be to program your brain neurons to ignore the training and maintain the status quo.

Or suppose that after completing the training you took the

attitude that it would not help you to correct your particular health problem. That expectation of failure also constitutes programming, and it would cancel out what you gained in the training, keeping you sick. Desire, belief, and expectation are the components of *faith*, the link between mind and brain that enables programs to be realized. The brain works both in the objective and subjective realms.

Take the bright college student whose father wants him to be a lawyer. He does not want to be a lawyer, but his father has a thriving practice and is respected in the community. So, encouraged by his father, the son becomes a lawyer. Does he prosper as his father has? No, because his efforts are half-hearted. That half-hearted quality affects his whole career. He becomes a mediocre lawyer.

Compare the son's desire with the father's motivation when he was a youth. The father had a burning desire to become a successful attorney. Despite financial obstacles and other problems, he applied himself and eventually succeeded. Desire, belief, and expectation set the stage for success in both the objective and the subjective worlds.

When Dr. Carl Simonton received a new patient, he showed that patient "before" and "after" pictures of former patients. "Now you see the cancer; now you don't." He was not bragging or selling himself by doing this. He was stimulating the patient's negative expectation and belief ("I'm a goner") to reverse themselves, becoming positive expectation and belief ("I, too, can be cured"). He usually showed these pictures, in the form of slides, to several patients at a time. He also insisted that patients' families see the slides. He wanted to change their expectations and beliefs about the patients' prognosis so they would communicate those expectations and beliefs to the patients, thereby reprogramming patients positively.

Belief turns on the mental computer by entering the message that "programming is on the way."

Belief also enables us to picture an end result with enthusiasm, and enthusiasm heightens the flow of energy that runs the computer. The brain then processes the information given to it by the believing mind. Its critical faculty has given the green light: "I will succeed."

When the second artificial-heart recipient sat up in his Louisville hospital bed only a few days after the implantation, the doctors were jubilant. One was quoted by the Associated Press as saying that the patient's "positive mental atttiude is a very important factor and a very strong factor in favor as far as recovery is concerned."

Reinforcement Procedure

The mind is the controller. So we benefit when we control the mind, thereby generating success with expectation and belief.

1. When you awake tomorrow morning, if you have to, go to the bathroom. Then go back to bed. Set your alarm clock to ring in fifteen minutes.
2. Close your eyes and roll them slightly upward toward your eyebrows (about 20 degrees).

I have analyzed the visualization process and have determined how it works best. Recall how people turn their eyes upward to find an answer to a question as if the answer were written on the ceiling or in the sky.

I have found that looking up in this manner triggers the brain to produce alpha rhythm. At the same time, looking upward and unfocusing the eyes in the process of looking away from any objects also triggers more right-brain activity.

The Mental Screen

Mind-control advantages occur best when the eyes are about twenty degrees above the horizontal. I call this area the mental screen.

Our use of the mental screen at the alpha level becomes an important means of improving our health.

With these explanations in mind, you can continue the procedure begun above:

3. Count slowly from 100 to 1. Do this silently—that is, mentally. Wait about one second between numbers.
4. When you reach the count of 1, hold a picture of yourself in your mind as youthful, radiant, healthy, and attractive.
5. Repeat mentally, "I will always maintain a perfectly healthy body and mind."
6. Then say to yourself, "I am going to count from 1 to 5. When I reach the count of 5, I will open my eyes, feeling fine and in perfect health, feeling better than before."
7. Begin to count. When you reach 3, repeat, "When I reach the count of 5, I will open my eyes, feeling fine and in perfect health, feeling better than before."
8. Continue your count to 4 and 5. At the count of 5, open your eyes and affirm mentally, "I am wide awake, feeling fine and in perfect health, feeling better than before. And this is so."

Eight Steps That Are Really Only Three

Go over each of the explanations of these eight steps below so that you understand its purpose while becoming more familiar with the sequence:

1. The mind cannot relax deeply if the body is not relaxed. It is better to go to the bathroom and then permit your body to enjoy full comfort. Also, when you first awake, you may not be fully awake. Going to the bathroom ensures that you wake completely. In case you are still not alert enough to stay awake, however, set your alarm clock to ring in about fifteen minutes, so that you do not risk beginning your daily schedule late.

2. As I explained, turning the eyes upward about twenty degrees triggers alpha rhythms in the brain and also causes right-brain activity. Later, when we do our mental picturing, it will be with our eyes turned upward at this angle. Meanwhile, this eye movement is a simple way to encourage alpha.
3. Counting backward is relaxing. Counting forward is activating. Counting 1, 2, 3 is like "get ready, get set, go." Counting 3 to 1 is pacifying; it takes you nowhere except deeper within yourself.
4. While relaxing, imagining yourself the way you want to be creates the picture. Hypochondriacs who relax and imagine themselves sick frequently create unwanted physical symptoms. You will do the opposite. Your mental picture will create *wanted* conditions—youth, health, and attractiveness.
5. Words repeated mentally, while you are relaxed, create the concepts they stand for. Pictures and words program the mind to make it so.

6, 7, 8. These last three steps simply involve counting to 5 to end your session. Counting upward activates you. But it is still good to give yourself "orders" to become activated at the count of 5. Do this before you begin to count, again along the way, and again as you open your eyes at 5.

When you wake up tomorrow morning and prepare yourself for the exercise, you will find that the eight steps are really three:

With your eyes turned upward twenty degrees:

1. Count backward from 100 to 1.
2. Picture yourself healthy and affirm your health.
3. Count up from 1 to 5, affirming good health and wide-awakeness.

Forty Days That Can Change Your Life

You now know what to do tomorrow morning, but what about after that?

Here is the program:

- Count backward from 100 to 1 for ten mornings.
- Then count backward from 50 to 1 for ten mornings.
- Then count backward from 25 to 1 for ten mornings.
- Then count backward from 10 to 1 for ten mornings.

After these forty mornings of countdown relaxation practice, count backward only from 5 to 1 and begin to use your alpha level for health benefits.

How to do this will be explained on the pages ahead. Keep reading as you practice, because there are health advantages you can enjoy even before the forty days are up:

- You can change your morning picture to help yourself with specific health problems.
- You can help others.
- You can expand your understanding of what your mind can do to solve problems and reach goals in other aspects of living.
- You can build up your belief and expectation and, therefore, improve your health-restoring ability.

If you follow this simple exercise each morning for forty days, you will acquire the ability to control your mind at the alpha level.

It may seem almost childish to lie there counting down this way. But each time you do, you reach a point of reference for the next time. You go deeper and deeper, slowing down your brain waves and bringing them under your control. This phrase, "under your control," means two things: (1) you are doing it purposefully, and (2) you are not falling asleep. This control, therefore, takes you to and keeps you at alpha, no deeper.

It helps to keep the procedure the same each morning: do the same steps at the same place and same time. The only thing that changes is the shift from 100 to 50 after ten practice mornings, and the subsequent shifts to 25, 10, and 5 every tenth morning after that. Adding other variables would blur the point of reference and possibly diminish your results.

What will the results be after forty days? You will be able to sit in a chair, count backward from 5 to 1 with your eyes turned upward, and program for

- more energy;
- greater enthusiasm;
- a productive day;
- improved health;
- optimism.

Session 3
Beginning to Help Yourself

1. Close your eyes and roll them slightly upward about twenty degrees toward your eyebrows.
2. Count slowly from 100 to 1. Do this silently—that is, mentally. Wait about one second between numbers.
3. When you reach the count of 1, hold a picture of yourself in your mind as youthful, radiant, healthy, and attractive.
4. Repeat mentally, "I will always maintain a perfectly healthy body and mind."
5. Then say to yourself, "I am going to count from 1 to 5. When I reach the count of 5, I will open my eyes, feeling fine and in perfect health, feeling better than before."
6. Begin to count. When you reach 3, repeat, "When I reach the count of 5, I will open my eyes, feeling fine and in perfect health, feeling better than before."
7. Continue your count to 4 and 5. At the count of 5, open your eyes and affirm mentally, "I am wide awake, feeling fine and in perfect health, feeling better than before. And this is so."

Good morning. Did you feel delightfully relaxed when you reached the count of 1?

As you practice each morning from now on, you will feel more and more relaxed. The whole process will become more familiar to you. You will become more comfortable with it. Comfort is the key to becoming relaxed.

As you practice your morning relaxation exercise, it will gradually become more automatic. After ten mornings, counting down from 50 to 1 will do as much for you as counting from 100 to 1. And after thirty more mornings, you will be a "professional relaxer," in control of the alpha level of mind, where picturing *creates*.

I could tell you all the ways you will be able to use the Silva Method by creating normal physical conditions through imagining—to erase spots on your lungs and eradicate a cough, to pass a kidney stone by imaging yourself crushing it in your fingers and then excreting it in the morning, to eliminate the swelling of arthritis by picturing yourself dusting powder from your knuckles. But my words probably will not sink in at this point. It is first-hand experiences that really sink in, so let me introduce you to Tag Powell, from Florida. Here in his own words is the story of his healing. Since the time he tells about here, he has become one of the most successful lecturers in the Silva Method.

Tag Powell's Story

I got osteomyelitis when I was fourteen. It's not a bone cancer, but is very much like it. In my case the deterioration of the bone was in the knee area. It was very mysterious how I got it—maybe it was unsterile operation conditions, maybe not. They loaded me with antibiotics, but these did no good. With normal osteo they give you antibiotics and it goes away.

I needed an operation about every three years. Doctors would go into the area, cut away the infected tissues, scrape out the osteo, and put things back together. It would be good for two or three years maximum; then they'd have to operate again. They tried radium treatments, shooting the radium into the leg to try to kill the germ. That only lasted about two years. They tried another system where they took the germ from the leg, shot it with radium, then put it back into my leg twice a week for six months. No luck. I tried every known osteo therapy.

Then I took the Silva course.

About six months after graduating from the Silva Method, my knee began to swell up. It was as big as a balloon, and I wound up on crutches. I used the Silva Method pain-control techniques to control the pain, but when something is swollen up that big, you invariably bump it on something (working in close quarters as I was at the time), and since you are not thinking about it at that time, you get highly intense pain.

I went to the local doctor and he wanted to send me to the University of Florida Medical Center in Gainesville, where they would cut my entire knee joint out, boil it for twenty-four hours, then freeze it for thirty days, and then put it back in. He said, "Maybe it will take." Maybe. With that weak kind of reassurance, as you can imagine, I didn't really want to go ahead with it. The system he recommended is actually used in extreme cases, usually only when the person is about to lose the leg. I asked for antibiotics for temporary relief and told him, "I'll think about it."

I went home. I couldn't get around and was lying in bed. The knee was swollen to about the size of a volleyball. I could not get my pants leg over it.

One night while lying there, I began to wonder: Do I really believe in the Silva Method? If so, then I could use it. This was early in 1978, about six months after I had graduated from the Basic Lecture Series.

So I went to level. I remembered that I had been told that the white blood cells could destroy the osteo. I remembered my visualization from class, and drew the white blood cells from various parts of my body. Starting with my toes, I mentally called the white blood cells to come to the knees. I was recruiting an army, picturing them coming to the battlefield.

When I got a whole army assembled into the right hip, I pretended to put them onto white horses with white shields and big white broad swords. When I got them all assembled and ready to go, I mentally yelled "Charge!" and pretended that waves of these creatures were riding in to the main area, fighting with broad swords and killing all the bad cells. The bad cells I visualized as skinny, dark, with skinny broad swords, skinny shields, not too effective.

I was sending in waves and waves, and was really getting into the visualization. Then I got the impression that we weren't winning, but were just holding our own. I thought, What does a doctor do? He scrapes it out. So I brought in a laser beam, just like the one in Star Wars. *I programmed the laser beam to hurt only the germs, not any white blood cells. I brought the laser beam down and aimed at the infected area.*

I was so into it at that time that I expected it to hurt when I aimed the laser beam at it, but it didn't. It felt a little warm, but that was all. I rotated the beam around, reaming out the knee just the way the doctor would do it when he was scraping. Then I backed the beam off. I was so exhausted with the pain and effort I just went to sleep.

The next morning I awakened and there was a ball of pus about the size of half a golf ball right in that area. About noon that day, that little pus sack broke and the drainage came out. The knee continued to get better.

I haven't had another problem since.

During the summer, after the psychic-mental-Silva operation, or whatever you want to call it, I went out with a group and for the first time in my life I played volleyball. Previously, if I'd played volleyball, I'd have ended up in the hospital.

I spent the whole day playing volleyball. When I went home that night, my leg hurt. My knee hurt. But it was a joyous feeling, because it was the muscles that hurt. I hadn't used those muscles since I was fourteen.

It continued to get better—better and better. I can now sit in a yoga position. I bought a pretty little red Sunbird, because I can get in and out of it. The real proof of the effectiveness of the cure was when I went to Egypt last year and climbed up and down the Great Pyramid. I could never have done that before. When we finished, I was totally physically exhausted, but the next day I was all right.

The programming took about thirty or forty-five minutes. My desire, belief, and expectation were strong at the time. It was almost a life-and-death situation, with the doctor wanting to freeze my knee for thirty days and all. I couldn't put it off.

I think the reason I did all the healing in one shot is that I realized I had to do it then. There was none of this business of "trying." I just had to do it. There was no "hoping" for it; they were going to cut off part of my leg if I didn't succeed.

That desire, that life-or-death type of need, gives you enough energy to achieve almost anything. If you can find a way to generate this kind of desire, you will reach your goals. I know, because I did it. My desire, coupled with a Silva Method technique applied at the alpha level, brought results.

Moving Down the Brain-Frequency Scale

What Tag Powell did for himself, others are doing daily for themselves with the Silva Method. Your ability to handle health problems for yourself and for others will gradually increase as your morning relaxation sessions become more and more effective.

The brain is an organ of healing. It runs the body. Too often it is used unconsciously as an organ of ailing. Between all the daily hassles and the major life crises, there is a world of disease-causing mental stresses out there.

The fact that we cannot identify which stressful event causes which unwanted symptom does not mean we cannot eliminate that symptom. Tag Powell did not identify the cause, way back in his youth, that was responsible for the advent of his knee problem. Still, he was able to use his mind to heal it.

As you continue to practice, you gradually acquire an automatic reflex. When stress comes, you insulate yourself from it, your attitude becomes more resilient, and stress affects you less and less. By using mental imagery, you may stop causing the original symptoms of the illness you are intending to relieve, but it is likely that other unwanted conditions will disappear as well.

Picturing With the Mind's Eye: Perhaps Our Greatest Gift

A pictures himself as weak and vulnerable to illness. He fears every germ and virus that is making the rounds. He imagines he is coming down with this sickness or that. He dreads approaching old age.

B pictures himself healthy and strong. Instead of holding pictures of illness in his mind, he pictures himself perpetually young, active, and attractive.

B will tend to live out his mental pictures and is the more likely of the two to enjoy a high level of good health. A, the hypochondriac, will also tend to live out his mental pictures, and will be affecting his body in ways that can produce very real discomfort and disease.

The mind's imagining faculty is a creative function. Nothing made by a human being could exist unless it started with a mental picture. That beautiful rose garden had to be imagined by the gardener. That painting had to be imagined by the artist. The chair you are sitting in had to be first pictured mentally by its creator before it could be sketched and then manufactured.

Ask yourself who mentally pictured the clothing you have on before it was sketched and the patterns made, or the building you are in before it was drawn in perspective, the plans and elevations drafted, the specifications written, and bids solicited from builders. Someone did the picturing, or these items would not be here. The imaging ability is humanity's creative power. It comes from within.

Nikola Tesla, an American electrical inventor early in this century who was far ahead of his time, was able to picture what he invented. In less than two months he was able to create from his imagination virtually all the types of motors and system modifications associated with his name. "The pieces of apparatus I conceived," he wrote, "were to me absolutely real and tangible in every detail, even to the minutest marks and signs of wear."

Tag Powell's mental picture of an army of white blood cells was just as real and tangible as Tesla's images. When he used the imaginary laser beam, he even expected it to hurt.

Imagining as if what you picture were real is a part of the success formula. When you reach the count of 1 and see yourself as vibrant and healthy in your morning practice session, you are actually creating what you imagine.

Be aware that your mental picture of yourself is the real you. The less-than-healthy situation you may now be experiencing is not normality but abnormality. The antidote is to desire the real you, to believe that you are restoring the real you, and to expect to succeed in changing yourself back to the real you.

Is it necessary to make diagrams and sketches before you visualize? Not at all. Indeed, the opposite is true: you would need to visualize before you could make diagrams and sketches. Tesla said that he observed to his delight that he could visualize with the greatest facility. He needed no models, drawings, or experiments and could picture the inventions all as real in his mind.

Each of us has an untapped reservoir of creativity. Slowing the brain waves is the means of tapping into it. As you slow your brain waves, you activate your right-brain hemisphere. The right hemisphere of the brain appears to be our connection to the creative realm, because with it we visualize what we want, thereby creating it.

Session 4
An Ounce of Prevention

1. Close your eyes and roll them slightly upward toward your eyebrows.
2. Count slowly and silently from 100 to 1. Wait about one second between numbers.
3. When you reach the count of 1, hold a picture of yourself in your mind as youthful, radiant, healthy, and attractive.
4. Repeat mentally, "I will always maintain a perfectly healthy body and mind."
5. Then say to yourself, "I am going to count from 1 to 5; when I reach the count of 5, I will open my eyes, feeling fine and in perfect health, feeling better than before."
6. Count. When you reach 3, repeat, "When I reach the count of 5, I will open my eyes, feeling fine and in perfect health, feeling better than before."
7. At the count of 5, open your eyes and affirm mentally, "I am wide awake, feeling fine and in perfect health, feeling better than before. And this is so."

You are now using one mental picture in your morning practice sessions: a picture of yourself as healthy. Later, if you have a health problem, you will be able to direct your creative energy visually, the way Tag Powell did to correct his health problem.

Meanwhile, though, it is important that you perfect your relaxation power so that you will be at the alpha level whenever you hold pictures in your mind. Even as you practice, you are helping to keep yourself healthy. Your morning mental picture of yourself healthy, repeated daily, is getting through, and in itself it can be strong medicine.

Take the case of Mrs. L.W., mother of two teenage boys.

This past year was a very negative one for me. One thing happened after another, my personality changed, and I became negative and depressed inwardly. I would try not to show it outwardly. I lost my self-confidence in several areas and began eating more and gaining weight. I was on diet pills and laxatives, which really weren't helping. My hearing became impaired. I had to use a hearing aid. I was worried about my husband and didn't know what to do. I wasn't as patient with our boys and yelled at them when they did something I disapproved of. Also, I was worried about our twelve-year-old, who is dyslexic, and concerned about his schoolwork.

I saw the Silva ad. I showed my husband and he went to the introductory lecture. He was very enthusiastic. I was still skeptical but agreed to attend.

It was the answer to my prayers.

I've found myself. I'm positive now, have peace of mind, awareness, no stress, and no pills. I'm on a sensible diet with plenty of exercise and have trimmed my weight and feel great. I'm excited about my improved hearing and know that very soon I won't need my hearing aids. I'm more patient with our sons and am getting better and better every day.

What was Mrs. L.W. heading for before she took the Silva course? It was clear that she was not maintaining her health but was gaining weight, having trouble with her bowels, and had developed a hearing impairment. Systems were going out of balance. More physical trouble seemed inevitable.

Enter the Silva Method. Her stress diminished and her systems became more balanced.

In your morning sessions, you are giving yourself a similar "tonic." You are getting a handle on your stress and paving the way for a higher level of health and well-being.

The brain has within it approximately thirty billion neurons, about three pounds of material in all. These neurons are like the components of a computer. Your computerlike brain is programmed to run your body, store your experiences and learning, and feed back this information to you on demand. It has been estimated that we are born with some two thousand separate programs in our mental computers, which are designed to run our bodies perfectly. The defects in these otherwise perfect programs are caused by stress, which begins almost the moment we are born.

Stress first affected your system when your mother suddenly disappeared from sight. Was that the second, third, or fourth day after you were born? No matter. Whenever it happened, it caused you anxiety. You were hungry and there was no food in sight. More anxiety. You had an irritated backside and there was no change in sight. More anxiety.

Anxiety is stress. Stress interferes with perfect programming. The greater the stress and the longer its duration, the more interference. Eventually, that interference wins out. Perfect programs become imperfect. The vital organs and essential systems of the body begin to function less than perfectly.

Stress, the Culprit

You could call the doctor, but after you do so use the Silva Method to defuse the stress and reprogram normally.

Fifty years ago doctors observed that anger caused a change in color of the stomach lining in a surgical patient. Now they have discovered that stress suppresses white blood cell activity. Acceptance of the fact that worry causes ulcers has been expanded to include the notion that nearly every bodily disorder is brought on by some stressful attitude, feeling, or emotion.

Do you get colds, headaches, aches, or pains? Have you ever had measles, whooping cough, mumps, or some of those other so-called contagious diseases? What about more painful or serious illnesses, such as cancer, gallstones, heart disease, or arthritis? All are triggered to a large degree by stress.

You will not receive what I am about to say joyously: it is you who are responsible for your illnesses. But don't judge yourself harshly for it. All humanity is making the same mistake. You and I have never been taught how to use our minds to eliminate stress, keep our immune systems alert, or keep our vital systems working harmoniously.

Overcoming Hidden Barriers

As you picture yourself in radiant health each practice session, the programming that may be interfering with your health is still present. Eventually, your new programming will replace it, but you can hasten this process by identifying the old programming and thus diffusing it. In identifying it, you come to understand and eliminate the cause of your health problems.

Here, in concrete terms, are the steps to eradicating the stress interfering with your health. In the morning session while you are relaxed but before you start picturing yourself healthy, ask yourself, "Why do I have this physical problem?" Let your mind wander. You will start to think about your sister, your mother-in-law, or your partner, your lawyer, your spouse, or your son or daughter.

Almost all stress stems from human relationships. If you can identify the stressful relationship that is "bugging" you, then you will have zeroed in on the cause and how to get rid of it.

Once you have identified the source, picture yourself shaking hands with or embracing the person in your imagination. Feel that you are "making up." Feel forgiveness—mutual forgiveness—flow between you.

In experiencing forgiveness what you are really doing is overcoming hidden barriers to your normal good health. Dissolve the friction through mental pictures and you dissolve the physical results of that mental friction.

Now go on to Step 4, picturing yourself healthy and affirming to yourself, "I will always maintain a perfectly healthy body and mind." Then go on to count from 1 to 5 and open your eyes.

To reiterate, I have added the following steps to your morning practice sessions. Let me list the new A, B, and C to Step 3:

3A. Ask yourself mentally, "Why do I have this physical problem?" Then let your mind wander.
3B. When you find yourself thinking about a certain person, picture that person.
3C. Picture yourself forgiving each other. Imagine a hug or a handshake, smiles, and heads nodding in agreement. Feel good about this.

You will find that your real-world relationship with this person has improved. You will have created a change, removed a silent barrier to health.

Deepening Your Alpha Level Through Muscle Relaxation

I have defined alpha level as being between seven and fourteen pulsations per second. As you relax in the morning by closing your eyes, turning them slightly upward, and counting backward from 100 to 1, you are lowering your brain-wave frequency toward this alpha range.

Some may reach this range within the first few practice sessions; others will take longer. There is no penalty for achieving alpha quickly, but for taking too long the penalty is a delay in the successful outcomes of your healing work.

This is a penalty nobody should want to endure. And it is not necessary to endure it. To guard against it, you can apply more methodology toward relaxing. Here is an additional exercise that accelerates the relaxation process. Perform it before beginning your countdown, to take yourself through a progressive relaxation. This is the process of turning your awareness onto different muscle groups in your body and relaxing them specifically. Usually you start at the top of your head and move all the way down to your ankles, feet, and toes. As you hold this book before you, eyes open, reading the instructions, actually perform progressive relaxation. Then, tomorrow morning you will be able to do it without the book.

First, turn your attention to your scalp. Let yourself feel it internally, consciously knowing it is there. This awareness might take the form of a tingling sensation or warmth. This is blood circulating in your scalp. If you relax your scalp, the blood will circulate even better. After relaxing your scalp, do the same with your forehead. Be aware of your forehead. Relax your forehead.

Relax your eyes. Feel their watery cushioning. Relax your jaw and mouth. Make your tongue comfortable in your mouth.

Relax your neck. Relax your shoulders. Relax your arms. Maybe the book will change position slightly as you do so, but read on.

Be aware of your chest and abdomen. Relax them. Relax your upper back and lower back.

Continue to become aware of the rest of your body, part by part, relaxing each in turn—your hips, thighs, knees, legs, ankles, feet, and toes.

Even though you are still reading, still mentally active, you should be able to feel the physical relaxation you have just induced. You will know what to do tomorrow morning to enjoy this same deep physical relaxation. You will use progressive relaxation just before you begin your countdown.

I will call this Step 2A. Because it takes a few minutes, I will make it optional. Do it tomorrow morning, but thereafter do it only when you have the time and inclination. Know that each time you do it, you will be taking out insurance—that you will be increasing the effectiveness of using your mind to heal yourself and help others help themselves.

In summary, here is Step 2A in your morning session:

2A. Starting with your scalp, focus your conscious awareness on the different parts of your body from head to toe, relaxing them as you go.

Session 5
Helping Your Doctor

1. Close your eyes and roll them slightly upward toward your eyebrows.
2. Count slowly and silently from 100 to 1. Wait about one second between numbers.
   A. Starting with your scalp, focus your conscious awareness on the different parts of your body from head to toe, relaxing them as you go.
3. When you reach the count of 1, hold a picture of yourself in your mind as youthful, radiant, healthy, and attractive.
   A. Ask yourself mentally, "Why do I have this physical problem?" Then let your mind wander.
   B. When you find yourself thinking about a certain person, picture that person.
   C. Picture yourself forgiving each other. Imagine a hug or a handshake, smiles, and heads nodding in agreement. Feel good about this.
4. Repeat mentally, "I will always maintain a perfectly healthy body and mind."
5. Say to yourself, "I am going to count from 1 to 5; when I reach the count of 5, I will open my eyes, feeling fine and in perfect health, feeling better than before."
6. Count. When you reach 3, repeat, "When I reach the count of 5, I will open my eyes, feeling fine and in perfect health, feeling better than before."
7. At the count of 5, open your eyes and affirm mentally, "I am wide awake, feeling fine and in perfect health, feeling better than before. And this is so."

Self-Care—No Substitute for Professional Care

Confidence in your physician, a relaxed attitude, and optimism regarding your cure are the three main factors in a climate for recovery.

Later, the mental procedures to help you cure any health abnormalities will serve as powerful tools for recovery. But these mental procedures will not be meant as a substitute for your physician's procedures. Rather, they will be ways to help your physician help you.

I recommend that Silva Method techniques, when used for health matters, always be done under the supervision of your health-care professional. He or she works in the objective dimension. You work in the subjective dimension.

Why is it necessary to use the subjective dimension at all? The answer is that when an intangible is causing a chemical imbalance, no tangible will permanently correct it. Intangible causes of chemical imbalances in the body are the stressful feelings, attitudes, and emotions discussed above. Relaxation and healing thoughts are what are needed to restore these imbalances. Until stressful feelings can be replaced by relaxed mental states, your physician can only help relieve the symptoms.

A businessman who worries and develops ulcers can be treated for those ulcers and get relief from the discomfort. But if he continues to worry, he continues to cause stomach ulcers. So, even with a skilled medical specialist on hand, much about your health depends upon you.

You and your doctor are a team.

Specific Ways to Help Your Doctor Help You

Medications, as prescribed by doctors, play an objective role in correcting physical problems. They work from outer toward inner levels. Mind plays a subjective role in correcting these problems. It works from inner levels of matter toward outer levels.

As soon as you take medication, you should enter the alpha level. Visualize the health condition and picture the medication going to where it has to go and doing what it is supposed to do.

When you do this, you are preparing the inner levels to respond in harmony with the outer levels. Healing is accelerated. The inner levels accept the medications for the correction of the health problems. Inner and outer pull together for your recovery.

Merely going to your alpha level whenever you have a health problem is therapeutic. I recommend that you go to alpha level three times a day when you are ill and stay there for fifteen minutes each time. The best times to do this are in the morning when you awaken, after lunch, and at night before falling asleep. These are times when you are most likely to be relaxed already and therefore able to function at alpha more productively.

The ideal patient for any doctor is a person who is mentally and physically relaxed and who is at alpha. In contrast to the person who is apprehensive, tense, and hyperactive, such a person makes optimal use of any medication.

Your Progress

You are now learning to control your physical activity, your brain activity, your awareness, your visualization and its ability to help detect health problems, and your right-brain hemisphere, with its ability to solve health problems. When you have a health problem, the alpha level helps to transfer it from the visible world of the body to the invisible world of the mind. The imagination can correct the problem in the invisible world of the mind and manifest it in the visible world of the body.

Controlling the alpha level and using the controlled imagination create health. You can achieve these controls now by doing your morning countdown and visualization exercises. When you have mastered control of your thoughts, you will be able to relax physically and mentally and find the center of the brain-frequency spectrum, where mind and awareness become attuned to the right-brain hemisphere. This hemisphere is the seat of imagination, which is creative energy in action. You create changes from the inner to the outer realm, and from the subjective to the physical realm.

Tomorrow morning, when you close your eyes, turn them slightly upward, and begin to count backward, you will be starting this sequence of events:

- Your body relaxes.
- Your mind relaxes.
- Your brain frequency slows down.
- Your right hemisphere is activated.

Then, when you begin to visualize yourself healthy—that is, when you begin to take an imaginary trip through your body, picturing all parts and organs working perfectly—another sequence of events will have started:

- Your picturing is accepted as a need.
- The subjective mind changes your energy body.
- The change in the energy body begins to manifest in the physical body.
- What you picture mentally becomes materialized and real.

Alpha—the relaxed level of mind that produces seven to fourteen brain pulsations per second and whose center frequency is ten—enables the mind to tune into both brain hemispheres, something it does not normally do at the wide-awake, or beta, level. At alpha, the mind has great power. It can detect health problems even before they fully manifest in the beta or outer physical dimension, and it can intuitively know that something needs attention. You can detect problems with the right hemisphere before it is possible to detect them with the left hemisphere. That is because the right brain operates at the *cause* level, the left brain at the *effect* level.

So, you can also help your doctor help you by suggesting possible preventive procedures. Your doctor may not necessarily confirm that these procedures are necessary, but when you alert your doctor to your conviction of their effectiveness, he or she may adopt a "Sure, why not?" attitude.

Session 6
Overcoming Stress

1. Close your eyes and roll them slightly upward toward your eyebrows.
2. Count slowly and silently from 100 to 1. Wait about one second between numbers.
   A. Starting with your scalp, focus your conscious awareness on the different parts of your body from head to toe, relaxing them as you go.
3. When you reach the count of 1, hold a picture of yourself in your mind as youthful, radiant, healthy, and attractive.
   A. Ask yourself mentally, "Why do I have this physical problem?" Then let your mind wander.
   B. When you find yourself thinking about a certain person, picture that person.
   C. Picture yourself forgiving each other. Imagine a hug or a handshake, smiles, and heads nodding in agreement. Feel good about this.
4. Repeat mentally, "I will always maintain a perfectly healthy body and mind."
5. Say to yourself, "I am going to count from 1 to 5; when I reach the count of 5, I will open my eyes, feeling fine and in perfect health, feeling better than before."
6. Count. When you reach 3, repeat, "When I reach the count of 5, I will open my eyes, feeling fine and in perfect health, feeling better than before."
7. At the count of 5, open your eyes and affirm mentally, "I am wide awake, feeling fine and in perfect health, feeling better than before. And this is so."

The Coming of Age in Stress Management

The outer physical world is the source of stress. The inner mental world is the source of stresslessness. Because it is in touch with the inner world, the right brain has a bonanza to offer the left brain and the stressful outer world. This bonanza is a means to manage stress.

Recently, the National Conference of Catholic Bishops commissioned a study of the health of priests in the United States. Some 4,600 priests took part in this first in-depth research of their health through a "self-perception" survey.

The study found that priests are subject to the same ailments that affect the rest of the population. However, even though they work longer hours, they have fewer sick days. They work well past the customary retirement age, and they live longer than other people, developing a state of serenity in their later years. Priests are meditative, and meditation is a mental state that insulates against stress.

Stress and Accident Frequency

Stress is the major cause of health problems, including accidents.

Stress is a killer.

If stress doesn't get us one way, it will get us in another. There is just no way you can coexist with stress.

People who go through an acutely stressful event often subsequently experience traffic accidents, falls, or other mishaps.

People who are chronically under stress often become accident prone.

The housewife in a hurry to prepare dinner (stressed by time) cuts her finger.

The teenager who hates to mow the lawn (stress) slashes a hand in the blade.

The man who is angry at his wife (stress) skids his car into a pole.

Stress reduces our equanimity and our awareness.

The more you use your alpha level, the more aware and in control you become. The knife does not slip. You stay clear of trouble. The steering wheel is under your skillful control.

How to Get Rid of Organic Disorders

Stress is the cause of health problems by whatever name we call them. Dealing with anxiety is better than dealing with kidney malfunction, because getting a problem solved at its root is better than letting it fester into a larger problem, which must be dealt with in turn.

People who make life-and-death decisions are under tremendous stress and experience great anxiety. Among such people, disease, depression, and other maladies are increasing. Air traffic controllers, law enforcement officers, statesmen—all are under killing pressure, and this hampers their decision making, slows their productivity, and puts a strain on their family and personal lives.

It is not sufficient to be able to relax "under fire." Even then, we can still be "burned." We must know how to use alpha to heal the burns. The burns are, of course, the illnesses and diseases that are so common today. To do this, we will now develop the ability to focus our attention on a particular health problem. We will then be able to concentrate on the solutions to that problem. This concentration is not the type of hard mental work we usually think of when we hear that word. No hands on chin and deeply furrowed brow. Far from it. Instead, the Silva Method helps us use the type of concentration that comes with a relaxed focus of attention, which allows more of our mind to be involved. In this state our ability to come up with the answer that will help us correct a particular health problem increases.

The Silva Method increases our ability to accept subjective experiences. We can make fuller use of feelings, images, dreams, and other internal pathways by which intelligence comes to us when we make health decisions.

The tragedy of modern humanity is that it is much too busy and that it does not find time to relax and reflect. When Dr. Carl Simonton began helping cancer patients at his Texas clinic, they arrived from all over the country for help. For the first step, patients attended an orientation session to learn about the procedures. When they heard that they were going to have to relax and use their imaginations, most of the patients left and went home, not wanting to take part in their own recoveries.

Fortunately for you, you are not of this frame of mind, or you would have left these pages quite a ways back. You are willing to take a few minutes in the morning to count backward to reach alpha.

If we were all to use our right hemispheres as the clergy does, we would all be able to live longer, more productive lives. Their time spent in prayer, meditation, and contemplation with their right brain enhances alpha frequencies. Their time spent in helping others also fosters the right brain's involvement.

There is a glimmer of hope in the world today. Perhaps people are becoming more meditative, more contemplative, and more prayerful as the benefits of going within are slowly being acknowledged. Still, the right brain needs a good public relations agent.

Stress management is being taught in more and more seminars. These are held under the sponsorship of business organizations, professional societies, hospitals, or private groups. They feature stress films and lectures. Their message is, "A little stress can do you good. A lot of stress can do you in."

These seminars provide participants with psychological questionnaires about themselves, which they can then compare with computerized stress profiles. This is all of interest to the left brain but not exactly therapeutic. The therapy these seminars provide comes in the tension-relieving exercises, deep breathing, and relaxation technique they teach. Some are even starting to present visualization techniques, with participants mentally picturing themselves as serene and passive. Some include positive affirmations while participants are in a relaxed state.

Somewhere in the chain of events leading up to these seminars, you may well find the Silva Method training. The impact of five million people who are stress-management experts cannot be denied. It is to be hoped that their effect on the rest of the world will continue. People will soon attend seminars to make themselves well. And then they will attend seminars to make other people well—all by using the stress-managing, inner-world, creative, healing right brain.

Preventive Steps to Bar Stress

The weakening of the immune system is believed to be a major cause of such serious illnesses as cancer, AIDS, leukemia, and other so-called incurable diseases. Whenever the immune system is weakened, life is threatened. What weakens the immune system? One answer to that question has been confirmed many times over. Stress!

Let us examine three major causes of stress.

1. *Guilt.* When you know that you are doing something wrong or something society believes is wrong, and you continue to do it, you are inviting a weakening of your immune system. Could this in part be a by-product of smoking?
2. A *deep loss.* When you lose something or someone of great value and are not able to recover that loss, you experience great stress, which, again, invites a weakening of your immune system.
3. *Working or living in a hated environment.* This is chronic stress. Chronic stress is known to cause a weakening of the immune system.

There are many other causes of stress. Their impact on your immune system may or may not be critical, depending largely on the amount of time involved and/or the importance. If you are waiting for the bus and are late for work, every second can be stressful, but in a few minutes the bus arrives. The temporary stress is not as likely to leave its mark on you. It has been said that if a man owes you a thousand dollars, that's his problem, his stress. But if that man owes you a million dollars, that's your problem, your stress. The bigger the problem, the greater the stress.

Knowing about these causes, what can you do about stress? The obvious answer is to behave in ways that will not cause you to feel guilty, to accept your losses philosophically, to make sure you work and live in a pleasant environment, and to solve small problems before they become big ones. This advice is easy to give, but not that easy to take or to apply. Life is not always so closely under our control.

But our minds are, or should be, under our control. With the Silva Method, you can mentally program yourself to change unwanted behavior. You can program yourself to accept your loss and to go into higher levels of material possession or relationships. And you can solve problems, big or small, at the alpha level. While awaiting the results of your programming, you can go to your alpha level three times a day for fifteen minutes and enjoy serenity, tranquility, and a "vacation" from stress while also strengthening your immune system.

The Effects of Negative Mental Pictures

If you have ever been confronted with the fangs of a poisonous cobra, merely imagining that event can cause your adrenaline to flow, your skin to perspire, and your heart to pound, as if the cobra were really present again. If you have ever been confronted with a jealous spouse, a snarling boss, or an incensed policeman, imagining the experience or worrying about it happening again can cause your hormones to speed up your body's functions as if you were in a real emergency. Your lungs pump faster. Your blood pressure rises. Your heart races. And your white blood cells, the body's combat troops in the battle against disease, are suppressed.

The more you concentrate on your fear or worry, the more harm you do to your body. In writing about people with cardiovascular disease, Dr. Dean Ornish of Harvard Medical School says, "When you are angry, worried, or afraid, your blood pressure and heart rate may increase dramatically, your arteries are more likely to go into spasm, and your platelets tend to clump together and clog up your blood vessels."*

Here are some commonly held mental pictures that cause unwanted body reactions:

- You are going to lose your job and have no income.
- You are going to have a heart attack or get cancer or some other serious disease.
- You will be attacked at night in the street.
- Your home will be ransacked and robbed.
- Your spouse will be unfaithful.
- You will lose your way.
- There will be a nuclear war.
- You will be alone in your old age.
- Something terrible will happen to a loved one.
- Your investments will drop in value or become worthless.

If you are a chronic worrier, you may be able to supply additional situations to this partial list.

How your body reacts to these mental pictures depends on how your past experiences cause you to feel. Your personal history programs your body's reactions to these fears. Your inability to cope with the stress caused by considering potential danger and your feelings of helplessness in the face of potential danger may lead to the following:

**Stress, Diet, and Your Heart* (New York: Holt, Rinehart and Winston, 1982).

- Depression
- Decrease in brain efficiency
- Suppression of the immune system
- Development of a disease syndrome

One of our researchers, Dr. Richard E. McKenzie, explains in an issue of the *Silva Newsletter* how the Silva Method can interrupt this sequence:

It provides for the growth and development of the awareness factor to identify stress and tension. It allows us to institute cognitive and perceptual controls to avoid a state of helplessness. It permits us to alter negative emotional response, such as depression.

And, finally, should medical intervention become necessary, it can improve the success of the treatment.

Belief in and Expectation of Illness

People who expect and believe that they have done something to make themselves ill can actually produce those illnesses.

Maybe you were told that sitting in a draft will make you contract a cold, and you accepted that statement as fact. Such acceptance makes it part of your belief system. The next time you sit in a draft, your belief will trigger the expectation of a cold. You know the rest of the story. The next time you sit in a draft, because you have reinforced the cause-effect relationship in your belief system, you are all the more certain that you will get a cold. And you do.

Viruses and germs are always present. They are held in check by our immune systems. But you can rein in or unleash your immune system with mental activity. Physicians are getting closer and closer to accepting the idea that the mind can make us well, but they have known for decades that the mind can make us sick.

Negative expectations make us sick. Positive expectations make us well. Both work equally well. When reinforced, these expectations get more and more effective. We can reinforce them by affirming them verbally or by hearing others affirm them verbally. Experiencing the results also reinforces these expectations, but so do visualization and imagination.

A person goes to see a physician. The physician listens to the problem, examines the patient, and writes out a prescription. The patient goes to a druggist, gets the prescription filled, and follows the instructions, perhaps "take two tablets every four hours." The patient recovers. What the patient does not know is that the doctor could not find anything wrong with the patient. The prescription was just for a sugar pill. But belief that the pill was medicine, belief that the physician prescribed the right medicine, and expectation that this medicine will fix the problem make the healing work. This is known as the placebo effect. The physician prescribes, knowing that the patient's own mind will do the job. And it does.

You, too, can harness this healing power of the mind to help others and yourself.

Session 7
Healing Others

1. Close your eyes and roll them slightly upward toward your eyebrows.
2. Count slowly and silently from 100 to 1. Wait about one second between numbers.
   A. Starting with your scalp, focus your conscious awareness on the different parts of your body from head to toe, relaxing them as you go.
3. When you reach the count of 1, hold a picture of yourself in your mind as youthful, radiant, healthy, and attractive.
   A. Ask yourself mentally, "Why do I have this physical problem?" Then let your mind wander.
   B. When you find yourself thinking about a certain person, picture that person.
   C. Picture yourself forgiving each other. Imagine a hug or a handshake, smiles, and heads nodding in agreement. Feel good about this.
4. Repeat mentally, "I will always maintain a perfectly healthy body and mind."
5. Say to yourself, "I am going to count from 1 to 5; when I reach the count of 5, I will open my eyes, feeling fine and in perfect health, feeling better than before."
6. Count. When you reach 3, repeat, "When I reach the count of 5, I will open my eyes, feeling fine and in perfect health, feeling better than before."
7. At the count of 5, open your eyes and affirm mentally, "I am wide awake, feeling fine and in perfect health, feeling better than before. And this is so."

Dr. Rupert Sheldrake, one of several scientists doing research in this area, believes in a field of intelligence that we all share, a phenomenon he refers to as a morphogenetic field. This field is reminiscent of Jung's collective unconscious. It may even be what is called Higher Intelligence. Initial experiments bear out the existence of this field, the possibility that it can be programmed by human experience, and that it in turn can program us. This latter activity would be identical with the mental activity that improves the health of ourselves and others.

Here is the simple formula for mental activity that you can use to help yourself and others:

1. Enter your alpha level.
2. Reinforce mentally and verbally your desire, belief, and expectation to help.
3. Back this up with visualization and imagination.

Let us examine these three steps in more detail.

First, close your eyes, turn them slightly upward, and count backward from 100 to 1.

Second, make affirmations mentally to yourself about your desires. If you are ill, mentally reaffirm your desire to get well. If a friend or relative is ill, mentally reaffirm your desire that he or she get well. Next, mentally affirm that this will happen—indeed, that it is already happening.

Third, mentally picture it actually happening. Do this in two steps: (1) visualize the afflicted area of the body, and (2) imagine this area changing back to normal. End your session.

Can there be anything simpler? Go to alpha; affirm your desire with belief and expectation; visualize the condition and imagine it healing. The whole process will take two minutes and cost you nothing. Isn't this something we should all be learning to do in kindergarten?

A Summary of Health-Producing Steps

Maintaining a negative mental attitude has always been known to produce negative physical conditions. Now we know that people who maintain a positive mental attitude rarely get sick.

But what *is* a positive mental attitude? There can be many answers to this question. For example, if you are a "good time Charlie," you have a positive mental attitude. There are many kinds of rose-colored glasses you can look through. However, though I applaud all kinds of optimistic viewpoints, not all of them are consistent with the Silva Method. This method involves three specific aspects of positive thinking: positive desire, positive belief, and positive expectation. These elements are the building blocks to better health; they form the mental climate we need to successfully apply the rest of the methodology.

Two Methods

The Silva Special Healing Method is used for health problems that are localized in the body. The Silva Standard Healing Method is used for general health problems and for persistent or stubborn localized problems. The Silva Special Healing Method comes under the heading of "laying on of hands." Neither is recognized by the medical profession as an orthodox method of therapy. Still, unorthodox, folklore, and holistic healing methods are becoming popular all over the world. The knowledge is getting around that some health problems that do not respond to conventional healing approaches do respond to holistic approaches. The laws affecting these holistic methods vary from country to country and state to state in accordance with their respective belief systems. Before you use the Silva Special Healing Method, be sure you are aware of any local restrictions about touching without a license.

For example, one day, while teaching some holistic techniques to Silva Method graduates in Buenos Aires, Argentina, I was about to demonstrate on a person. But one of those present warned me that laying on of hands was illegal in Argentina.

"Today's session ends at seven P.M," I announced. "I will stay an extra hour to teach these techniques to doctors only."

Twenty-seven doctors in the class stayed on to learn the

methods. At the end of the instruction session, one doctor said, "I was in an automobile accident nine months ago and suffered a whiplash. I have been treated with everything known to medicine, yet I still suffer the pain. I have it right now. Will these techniques work on me?"

"This is a good time to find out," I replied.

Another doctor volunteered to apply the technique. I went over the steps with him again. He performed the special hand application, which takes only three to five minutes. When he was finished, I asked the doctor/patient to check himself, which he did thoroughly, moving this way and that. Finally, he blurted out, "A good ninety percent of the pain is gone. You know, this thing really works!"

Earlier in the day we had discussed the fact that the same energy used in laying on of hands is at work when Uri Geller of Israel bends spoons with his mind. I reminded the doctor that the spoon continues to bend on its own after Geller puts it down. "Don't be surprised if, by tomorrow morning, the pain is completely gone."

No sooner had we assembled the next day when this doctor stood up. "The pain is completely gone." He received applause. Pain, chronic or acute, is not our heritage, nor is disease of any kind. Perfect health is our heritage. We need to claim it.

Our human capabilities to make ourselves sick have been thoroughly exploited. Our hospitals are big business. Pharmaceuticals are a growth industry. The cost to individuals and to state governments is enormous. The cost to the federal government is preposterous. But our human capabilities to make ourselves well and stay well have barely been touched. They are only just beginning to be recognized. The millions of Silva graduates are just a drop in the bucket of humanity. Every person needs to become aware of his or her ability to self-heal and to heal others.

Session 8
Man, the Healer

1. Close your eyes and roll them slightly upward toward your eyebrows.
2. Count slowly and silently from 100 to 1. Wait about one second between numbers.
   A. Starting with your scalp, focus your conscious awareness on the different parts of your body from head to toe, relaxing them as you go.
3. When you reach the count of 1, hold a picture of yourself in your mind as youthful, radiant, healthy, and attractive.
   A. Ask yourself mentally, "Why do I have this physical problem?" Then let your mind wander.
   B. When you find yourself thinking about a certain person, picture that person.
   C. Picture yourself forgiving each other. Imagine a hug or a handshake, smiles, and heads nodding in agreement. Feel good about this.
4. Repeat mentally, "I will always maintain a perfectly healthy body and mind."
5. Say to yourself, "I am going to count from 1 to 5; when I reach the count of 5, I will open my eyes, feeling fine and in perfect health, feeling better than before."
6. Count. When you reach 3, repeat, "When I reach the count of 5, I will open my eyes, feeling fine and in perfect health, feeling better than before."
7. At the count of 5, open your eyes and affirm mentally, "I am wide awake, feeling fine and in perfect health, feeling better than before. And this is so."

As you learn in your forty-morning countdown training to go to your alpha level, you are gaining control of the ten-cycle brain frequency, a level of mind formerly considered to be the subconscious. You are learning to use the subconscious consciously.

What I learned early in my research was that this is also the psychic, or clairvoyant, dimension. The right hemisphere, which is the intuitive, creative, and psychic part of our brain, is used at this brain frequency.

We find that only about ten percent of humanity is naturally clairvoyant. Clairvoyant people's use of both hemispheres in their thinking forms a life-style. These people become "prophets and wise men." They are able to "cure the sick, raise the dead, cleanse the lepers, and cast out devils."

You are training yourself to be a healer.

We all have the need to help each other. When you help another person, you are better able to help yourself. There are two healing methods that you can use to help another person with a health problem while you train. Both require you to be at your alpha level for optimum results. But even though you are only partway through your training, you can already reach a sufficiently deep level of mind to add your healing energy to that of an ailing person. That increment of energy could make a decided difference. It might be the difference between ailing or healing.

The Silva Special Healing Method

The methods of healing I mentioned previously, which involved the laying on of hands, are illegal in Argentina but legal in Brazil. In Brasília, the capital of Brazil, I demonstrated the special method on a young girl who could not bend her left leg as far as she could bend her right leg. Right after the three-minute application, she could bend her left leg just as far as the right leg.

In Puerto Alegre, Brazil, the technique was applied in front of a large gathering of Silva Method graduates on a woman who had suffered a fall and had hurt her neck. She had worn a neck brace for a year and a half, and without it she could not hold her head up; her head would fall forward or to the side. After the Silva Special Healing Method was applied, the brace was removed. She was asked to test herself. She tilted her head to the back, forward, and to the sides. The audience applauded. She exclaimed loud enough for all to hear, "Now I can drive a car!"

In Guayaquil, Ecuador, a graduate came forth to be healed by this technique. A medical doctor taking the training volunteered to apply it. The patient had been in an accident and had damaged three vertebrae at about the waist level. The patient could not bend forward more than twelve inches, because the surgeons had fused the vertebrae together. However, after the doctor applied the technique, the man bent to the floor. After the deafening applause had subsided, the doctor announced, "That could not have been done with conventional medicine."

What you are about to learn may or may not be legal in your state or country. It is best to check with local authorities before applying it.

The two techniques described below and in the next chapter are the Silva Special Healing Method and the Silva Standard Healing Method. The first to be described, the Silva Special Healing Method, is for use where the health problem is localized in some relatively small area of the body. The second, the Silva Standard Healing Method, is for use both where the health problem is more general and where the localized problem is particularly stubborn.

Special Vibration Frequency of the Healing Hand

To use the Silva Special Healing Method, you need to learn hand vibration. Hand vibration is a rapid motion—ten vibrations per second—of the hand. You can practice hand vibration on a flat table or desk top. Holding your hand so that your fingertips touch the surface, vibrate your hand at approximately ten cycles per second (CPS) while your fingertips maintain contact with the surface of the table. Using the second hand of your watch, count the vibrations as you watch the seconds go by. You should be able to maintain ten vibrations per second.

This hand-vibration technique will help the healer to function at a brain frequency of ten cycles per second. When the healer vibrates the hands at this frequency, there is a feedback to the healer's brain that helps it to function at ten cycles per second. When the healer's brain functions at ten cycles per second, the energy field of the brain and body, sometimes known as the aura, is encouraged to vibrate at this frequency. If another person is within this energy field, that person's aura can be caused to vibrate sympathetically at ten cycles per second. When you are able to vibrate your hands at ten cycles per second, you are ready to apply the Silva Special Healing Method.

The Method

Place the tips of the fingers of your right hand on the left side of the patient's head, spreading the fingers so they touch and cover the area of the patient's left-brain hemisphere. Place the left hand over the right side of the patient's head in the same manner, spreading the fingers to cover the right-brain hemisphere. Spreading the fingers not only increases the area that is covered but also projects the energy rather than "short-circuiting" it back to your own body.

When the fingertips of both hands are in contact with the patient's head, both healer and patient should close their eyes. The healer takes a deep breath, holds it, bows the head, and then starts to vibrate the hands. While holding the breath and vibrating the hands, the healer recalls how it feels to be in the relaxed alpha level. The healer keeps in mind that the vibration is being done to correct the cause of a problem in the patient that the healer is aware of.

The healer continues until he or she has to breathe again. Then, just before taking a breath, the healer removes the hands from the patient's head. The healer opens his or her eyes and lightly rubs the palms of the hands together until breathing is normalized. The patient keeps his or her eyes closed.

After breathing is normalized, the healer repeats the cycle. This time the fingertips of the left hand are placed on one side of the afflicted area and those of the right hand go on the other side. The healer vibrates the fingers. When the healer must breathe, he or she removes the hands from the afflicted area and rubs them together until breathing is normalized. Then the healer repeats the head application.

For problems in the head area, such as headaches, the healer applies one application on the head while standing in front of the patient. The healer takes a deep breath and holds it, just as in the previous applications. Next, the healer stands behind the patient and applies one application from the back of the patient's head. Now, instead of holding the breath with lungs full of air, the healer holds the breath with lungs empty of air. The healer continues to vibrate the hands at ten vibrations per second and again recalls how it feels at the relaxed alpha level. Then the healer repeats the front application as before, with lungs full of air, to complete the healing.

When contacting the patient's head with the fingertips, the healer starts vibrating the hands as soon as his or her eyes are closed. An application with the lungs full is called a *positive application.* An application with the lungs empty is called a *negative application.* Negative applications are done only to the back of the head and only in the healing of head problems. Applications for correcting any other kind of health problems are positive.

In making applications, the healer must always be at a relaxed level and must keep in mind that the applications are being done to correct the *cause* of the problem in the healer's mind—namely, the patient's problem.

When a healer vibrates his or her hands at the rate of ten vibrations per second, an anesthetizing and sterilizing effect takes place. If the patient has an open, bleeding wound, the healer vibrates the hands over it while imagining the bleeding stopping and healing taking place. As reinforcement to these thoughts, the healer should say aloud, "No pain, no bleeding." In response, the pain and bleeding usually stop.

A Review of the Silva Special Healing Method

Again, this method is useful in helping another person recover from a localized condition. Your ability to go to the alpha level is recommended but not required.

1. Relax and affirm your desire for and your belief and expectation that healing will take place.
2. Place your hands over the subject's head—left hand over right hemisphere, right hand over left—with fingers spread. Vibrate your hands at ten vibrations per second.
3. When you need to breathe, stop and rub your hands while normalizing your breathing.
4. Then repeat the vibrations, one hand on each side of the subject's affected area.
5. Then repeat the vibrations over the subject's head, left side and right, as in Step 2.
6. End your relaxation.

Note: Always rub your hands before, after, and between applications of vibrations.

In the case of bleeding or hemorrhaging, vibrate your hands within three inches over the affected area, mentally picturing the stoppage of the bleeding and saying aloud, "No pain, no bleeding."

The Ethics of Healing Ourselves and Others

It would seem that there could be no argument with better health. Yet we occasionally run into criticism on an ethical, moral, or religious level. Some feel that illness bears within itself a lesson to be learned and that if we heal ourselves we deprive ourselves of a learning experience. Similarly, in this view, if we help someone else to heal, we deprive that person of a learning experience. Others say that the mind power we use to heal comes from the devil; still others say that we are trespassing on forbidden ground.

We find in Jesus's teachings the answers to all of these challenges. No, I am not trying to convert anyone to Christianity, but neither do I desire to be pressured into accepting someone else's viewpoint.

I believe that our Creator is perfect and all-encompassing, and that there is no power that is not His. Abnormalities are created by humanity going contrary to nature. Corrections of those abnormalities result from working with nature.

When Jesus healed, religious leaders of His time said He was in league with the devil. Later, St. Paul spent a good portion of his ministry trying to get people in the churches he established to quit bickering about who had the most power, who was best, and who was most right, but to get on with the task assigned by Jesus: to heal the sick, raise the dead, cast out demons, and teach others to do the same.

Jesus said, "By their fruits ye shall know them." Silva graduates are dedicated to correcting problems and making this planet a better place to live.

If humanity's fruits were bad, we would not last.

We have lasted.

We can all live longer and happier lives using more of our minds. This is ethical, moral, and religious. Still, the Silva Method is not a religious movement, nor is it a movement into the occult.

There is nothing secret about our organization, nothing dramatic. It has no rituals, no initiations. The Silva Method simply seeks to acquaint people with the potential of the whole person and to show them how, by using more of the mind, they can rid themselves of limited ways of thinking and unproductive habits and move on to higher and higher levels of creativity, enjoyment, and success.

Session 9
Healing Energy

1. Close your eyes and roll them slightly upward toward your eyebrows.
2. Count slowly and silently from 100 to 1. Wait about one second between numbers.
   A. Starting with your scalp, focus your conscious awareness on the different parts of your body from head to toe, relaxing them as you go.
3. When you reach the count of 1, hold a picture of yourself in your mind as youthful, radiant, healthy, and attractive.
   A. Ask yourself mentally, "Why do I have this physical problem?" Then let your mind wander.
   B. When you find yourself thinking about a certain person, picture that person.
   C. Picture yourself forgiving each other. Imagine a hug or a handshake, smiles, and heads nodding in agreement. Feel good about this.
4. Repeat mentally, "I will always maintain a perfectly healthy body and mind."
5. Say to yourself, "I am going to count from 1 to 5; when I reach the count of 5, I will open my eyes, feeling fine and in perfect health, feeling better than before."
6. Count. When you reach 3, repeat, "When I reach the count of 5, I will open my eyes, feeling fine and in perfect health, feeling better than before."
7. At the count of 5, open your eyes and affirm mentally, "I am wide awake, feeling fine and in perfect health, feeling better than before. And this is so."

The Silva Standard Healing Method

Centuries ago, Mesmer made sweeping passes with his hands. These were called mesmeric passes. They have also been called magnetic passes and healing passes. The ancient Hawaiian *kahunas,* or healers, used similar passes to cleanse the aura of impurities.

Today, we know that these passes with the hands involved an energy transfer. This energy transfer involved the mind as well as the hands. The mind controls and directs the energy transfer.

Point the fingers of your right hand at your left palm. Keep the fingers at least a foot away from your palm, so you do not feel heat energy. Now slowly move the fingers of your right hand up and down, still pointing them at your left palm; move them slowly, so you do not fan the air. You will detect something going up and down your palm. It will feel like heat or air, but it will be neither. What you will feel will be energy, the same energy used in the healing process. Many scientists are beginning to call this energy psychotronic energy.

The Silva Standard Healing Method involves the use of this energy, a physical energy applied with passes made with the hands. However, because the mind controls and directs this energy, the mind must be in a relaxed state and must focus on the problem with a sincere desire to heal.

The immediate effect in the subject is that of an anesthetic: pain disappears. But another phenomenon is detected as well: a sterilization of the area appears to take place, and open wounds there do not become infected.

Here is the basic procedure. The subject is seated or is in a horizontal position, keeping his or her eyes closed during the entire process. The healer goes to the alpha level and mentally expresses a desire for the subject's healing. The healer makes sweeping passes from the subject's head to the toes.

When the subject's whole body has been subjected to the sweeping passes, the healer places his or her hands a few inches from the subject's head, one hand over the forehead and one at the back of the head. After a few moments, the healer changes the position of the hands to the sides of the subject's head. The healer then places his or her hands at the upper chest and back, directing mental healing thoughts to the body's immune system. Finally, if there is a localized health problem, the hands are placed at this part of the body, and healing is mentally directed there.

The Scientific View

In its April 1984 issue, *Science Digest* published an article entitled "The Mind as Healer." This article asked the question, "Can simple thoughts heal the body?" and covered work done by scientists and researchers in such organizations as the National Institutes of Health, the Institute for the Advancement of Health, George Washington University, and Harvard Medical School. The goals were to aid in understanding the relationship between mental stress and immune system weakness and to explore the role of positive mental imagery in activating the immune system's response. But the work reported by these scientific bodies was not conclusive. Do we have to await their outcomes in order to use simple mind techniques? I hope not. I hope all who read this book will begin to use the mind to make and keep themselves well without demanding full understanding and total acceptance by the scientific and medical communities.

Meanwhile, I can offer my own scientific explanation of why positive mental imagery benefits health. All objects, including the human body, radiate and transmit energy. Moreover, everything objective, including energy fields, has a counterpart in the subjective dimension—that is, in consciousness. The radiation of objects interacts with the electromagnetic-chemical energy on the subjective dimensions.

When humans function in the objective (twenty-cycles-per-second brain frequency) dimension, human thoughts modulate objective radiation alone. When humans function in the subjective (ten-cycles-per-second brain frequency) dimension, human thoughts modulate both subjective and objective radiation.

Inanimate matter, or objects, radiate an overall static (fixed) field that can be altered by light radiation and thought-modulated human auras. Modulating an energy field, whether objective or subjective, means adding to or subtracting from a static field. That means that something, or some intelligence, is contained in the modulation of the field. Animate matter radiates a varying field that can be altered by light radiation and by human auras.

Distant Effects With Alpha

When humans function in the objective dimension with an intention of influencing matter, they are able to influence both inanimate and animate matter within a certain limited distance. When humans function in the subjective, or clairvoyant, dimension with an intention of influencing matter, they are able to influence inanimate matter within a certain limited distance; they can also influence animate matter for an unlimited distance.

The human body functions as both a frequency divider and a frequency multiplier. Regardless of what frequency the brain is functioning on—whether at twenty cycles per second (in the objective dimension) or ten cycles per second (in the subjective one)—and regardless of which brain hemisphere we are using to do our thinking, the body is producing subharmonics of this fundamental frequency—that is, smaller divisions of it—while producing multiples of the fundamental. One of the multiplied frequencies falls within the infrared range. Humans are always automatically registering or recording information consciously or subconsciously on inanimate and animate matter in the environment.

Humans who desire to do so can learn to act as clairvoyants by functioning *consciously* on the subconscious. Further, they can learn to record information at will on animate matter nearby or far away, on inanimate matter nearby, and even on distant inanimate matter through another person in the remote environment. The latter is known as a "repeater effect."

The Mind as Miracle Healer

Residents of a small island in the Fiji group once called themselves the only people who could walk on glowing embers, but nowadays this feat is understood to be universally possible. Thousands of people in all walks of life, with all levels of education, and from various races and cultures have firewalked. Some seminars for building the self-image teach participants to walk on fire in only one day or less. These involve a type of hypnotism.

What is actually happening during firewalking? How can a certain mental act keep the human skin unaffected by searing heat? The laws of physics seem to be broken in this phenomenon and there is no scientific explanation. The only plausible answer is that the mind has the ability to change the molecular structure of human flesh.

One noted healer, Olga Worrall, was found to have changed the spectroscopic profile (a molecular analysis by color) of water by holding samples in her hand for twenty to thirty minutes.* Such a test indicates that the water underwent a change in molecular structure. Since our bodies are seventy to eighty percent water, it is not hard to see, in the context of this example, that a diseased cell might indeed be changed into a healthy cell by such contact.

Many questions simply have no answers. What part does energy play in such transformations? How is energy directed by the mind? What is the role of belief, of faith, of prayer? Are there factors involved of which we are not yet aware? Shall we just "do our thing" and let people call it a miracle?

One day, many years ago, a friend came to see me in my office.

*Coauthor Robert Stone was at the Second World Psychotronic Conference in Monte Carlo in 1975 where these results were discussed.

He told me his brother, a city official, was dying.

"But I talked with your brother only two days ago," I said.

"That night," my friend told me, "he felt very bad and went to the hospital. They found that his kidneys had stopped functioning, and the hospital could not get a dialysis machine." At that time, only a few hospitals had dialysis equipment. There was a dialysis machine in a San Antonio hospital, he told me, but it was scheduled for use on another patient. Meanwhile, the sick man had lapsed into a coma due to urea poisoning in his brain.

As soon as my friend left the office, I went to the hospital. I got there very quickly, as the hospital is only six blocks from my office. I had to enter through the emergency entrance, because if a doctor had seen me entering through the front door, he would have called the police to run me away. The medical profession did not take easily to my methods, as I will explain in a later chapter.

When I got to the room of the sick official, his mother and sister were present. I told them a little white lie: I said I was sent by the Cursillo movement, a Christian teaching organization, to pray for him. It was true that I once belonged to that movement, but I did not at that time.

The mother told me that the doctors had tried all day to bring her son out of a coma but had failed. They now had little hope that he would live.

"Excuse me," I said. "I will now say my prayers."

I stood on the patient's right side, next to the bed, and went into my meditation-concentration (my clairvoyant) level. I pretended someone was listening to what I was saying mentally: "This man is thirty-four years old. He has a big, strong body, and there is much work to be done on this planet. I don't believe it justified that because his kidneys have stopped functioning he has to go. All his other organs, glands, and systems are young and functioning well. Why not give us a chance to get his kidneys to function again?"

While I was mentally asking this question, our sick official sat up in bed, looked at me with the eyes of a sleepwalker, the whites of his eyes yellowed with the urea poisoning. He recognized me and said, "Hi, José. What are you doing here?"

"What are you doing here?" I answered.

"Where am I?" he responded.

"You are in the right place," I answered. "Close your eyes, go back to sleep. Everything is going to be all right."

He closed his eyes, fell back on the pillow, and appeared to go back into a coma.

The mother told her daughter to run and get the doctor and tell him what had happened. As soon as she said that, I thought, I had better run, too.

Two hours later, the sick official started to pass urine. His kidneys started to function normally. Years later, they were still functioning normally.

A Review of the Silva Standard Healing Method

1. Enter the alpha level.
2. Affirm your desire for and belief and expectation that healing will take place.
3. With the subject in a prone position and the subject's eyes closed, make sweeping passes with your hands over his or her body from head to toe.
4. For a few moments, hold your hands over the subject's head, forehead, back, and sides of head, then over the chest and back (thinking of the immune system), and then over any localized problem area, each time visualizing the problem and imagining a correction taking place.
5. End your alpha session.

A Fundamental Formula for Helping Yourself and Others

This three-step formula contains the fundamental steps for any healing event in which the Silva method is used.

1. Go to alpha.
2. Reinforce your desire for and your belief and expectation that conceptualizing and verbalizing will heal.
3. Visualize the unwanted condition and imagine it changing to normal.

Using the Silva Method

At whatever stage you are in with your alpha-producing morning countdown exercises, you can now program yourself to make the Silva Method work successfully for you time after time. This approach involves the above fundamental formula, applied not to healing but to your ability to trigger healing.

First, go to alpha.

Next, using words that occur naturally to you, mentally affirm your desire for the ability to make and keep yourself well and to help others to do the same through the control of your mind.

Finally, visualize yourself doing countdown exercises, vibrating your hands, or making passes with your hands. Then imagine yourself healthier and imagine others smiling as you help them become healthier.

Do it now.

Session 10
Desire, Expectation, and Belief

1. Close your eyes and roll them slightly upward toward your eyebrows.
2. Count slowly and silently from 100 to 1. Wait about one second between numbers.
   A. Starting with your scalp, focus your conscious awareness on the different parts of your body from head to toe, relaxing them as you go.
3. When you reach the count of 1, hold a picture of yourself in your mind as youthful, radiant, healthy, and attractive.
   A. Ask yourself mentally, "Why do I have this physical problem?" Then let your mind wander.
   B. When you find yourself thinking about a certain person, picture that person.
   C. Picture yourself forgiving each other. Imagine a hug or a handshake, smiles, and heads nodding in agreement. Feel good about this.
4. Repeat mentally, "I will always maintain a perfectly healthy body and mind."
5. Say to yourself, "I am going to count from 1 to 5; when I reach the count of 5, I will open my eyes, feeling fine and in perfect health, feeling better than before."
6. Count. When you reach 3, repeat, "When I reach the count of 5, I will open my eyes, feeling fine and in perfect health, feeling better than before."
7. At the count of 5, open your eyes and affirm mentally, "I am wide awake, feeling fine and in perfect health, feeling better than before. And this is so."

The Miracle Makers: Desire, Belief, Expectation

You can change your life no matter what. Consider this testimony by Ed Thiessen:

Six years ago, if you would have told me I would ever be happy and healthy, I wouldn't have even smiled at the thought. My health was so bad I couldn't even imagine being well.

That was before someone introduced me to the Silva Method and the power of the mind.

When I was born in 1962, I wasn't expected to live, but if I did it was predicted that I would have severe brain damage and cerebral palsy. It was later found out, through further examination, that I had muscular dystrophy as well. I was also partly deaf, had severely crossed eyes, and was legally blind.

The "experts" didn't give my parents much hope I would ever be able to read or write or function in the "outside" world—outside of a state institution. Because of this and my declining health, they didn't expect me to live for long.

At the age of two I had my first surgery on my eyes to correct my vision and my crossed eyes.

From 1967 to 1979 I was placed in institutions and special schools and went through several operations on my legs and eyes to try to correct my many problems. But none seemed to really help. My eyesight, hearing, and speech were getting worse.

Then, in the early part of 1978, a volunteer gave me a book she had been reading. I often looked at books to see how many words I knew. As I read and reread your book many times, over a period of time I mastered the techniques in the book. At times I even slept with the book. I wore the book out.*

The doctors couldn't understand it, but my health seemed to be getting better. I did not tell them what I was doing—it's called "programming."

First I began walking. In a short time I no longer needed braces

**The Silva Mind Control Method* (New York: Simon & Schuster, 1977).

for my legs and arms. My hearing was restored, as well as my speech.

They said I would lose my eyesight, but, after I went to level three to four times each day, my eyesight improved. In the early part of 1980 I was able to leave the institution for good.

A few months later my aunt heard about Silva Mind Control, and she thought it would help me. She did not know how much it had helped me already. In December of 1980 we took the class.

The class helped me even more. My health improved greatly. In 1981 I stopped wearing glasses, and now I have 20/20 vision and am in perfect health.

In 1982 I took my GED test for my high school diploma and only missed one question, in trigonometry. That was because I did not program for the problem.

I used to have to buy two pairs of shoes for every one I needed, as my feet were not the same size. I programmed at the beginning of last year (1983); now both feet are the same size. One foot grew three sizes in less than one year.

All that is left from the past is a slight limp. That will pass soon. That is one of my projects for 1984.

My success is not a "miracle," and I didn't do what I did because I am a super-special person. What I did, I believe anyone can do. It just takes belief, a method (Silva), and a lot of work.

One day people will be so firmly in control of their minds that desire will be sufficient to trigger the manifestation of their expectations. Methodology will no longer be necessary. It is certain that my desire for the city official to heal and my expectation and belief that he *would* heal were key elements in his healing, as was my mental image of him as healed.

These concepts are difficult for scientists to accept. Thoughts, feelings, and other forms of mental activity are not measurable in ordinary ways and are therefore not subject to scientific study and explanation. But if you analyzed *desire* by first studying the meaning of the word, you can see it as the turning on of the computer. When the computer is turned on, then *expectation* proclaims the advent of a solution, and belief—based on all the previous solutions obtained by the computer and the infallibility of the programming—produces the desired result. It is possible that desire, expectation, and belief actually permit our minds to function in the way they were designed to function, and that without these elements normal mental functioning is blocked.

Your daily morning sessions enable you to reach your creative level of mind quickly and easily, because you *desire* the health advantages and other problem-solving advantages and mental abilities that this level of mind brings to you. You practice, because you believe you can do more with your mind than you are now doing and because you expect your desire to be fulfilled.

Thus, your practice is actually a form of computer programming. Your computer is plugged in and turned on (desire). Your computer has the appropriate circuits to handle this job (expectation). Your computer produced before and it will produce again (belief). You are succeeding. Desire that success. Believe you are attaining it. Expect it.

At Alpha, Healing Is a Natural Effect

If you know how to enter alpha and somebody who is ill does not have this ability, you are in a position to help this person. It is as if this person has fallen in the well and you have a rope to throw.

Let us call the ill person A and the healthy person who can go to alpha *B*. And let us say that *B* comes within the energy field of A—that is, within a few feet.

B can go to alpha, place his or her hands over the affected area of A, and imagine the illness disappearing and wellness taking its place. At that moment, an energy interchange is occurring. It is as if a healing energy has left the hands of *B*, entered A, and corrected the problem.

Kirlian photography, invented in the Soviet Union, actually allows us to see such an interchange. One places one's hands on light-sensitive paper—usually standard photographic paper—in a dark room. A high-voltage field is briefly activated, and when the paper is developed an image appears of an energy field around the fingers and hand. This energy field is diminished directly after a healing by the laying on of hands, but after a few seconds it is fully restored.

It is important that *B's* hands do not touch each other when applied over *A's* affected area. This would be like short circuiting the energy.

Alpha Suggestions

Your right brain energy is stronger at alpha, which makes visualizing more potent. When you visualize strongly, you direct energy to create normality.

Mesmer, Braid, Freud, Jung, Adler, and Coué all believed in the power of suggestion. Mesmer saw this power as magnetism at work, and later the power was actually called Mesmerism. Braid called it hypnotism. But it was French psychologist Emile Coué who used direct suggestion. He had his subjects look at themselves in a mirror and repeat frequently each day, "Every day in every way I'm getting better and better."

Suggestion is used to strengthen expectation and belief. If you are at alpha when suggestions are made, both brain hemispheres are creating the goal. Therefore, stronger impressions are made at alpha and more creative energy goes to work.

Though Coué was not aware of alpha brain frequencies, his method incorporated them. When functioning at a nonrelaxed, or beta, level, the brain frequency dips into alpha thirty times a minute but each such dip lasts only microseconds. Add up these microseconds and they total a few seconds during each minute. Saying the Coué affirmation a hundred times a day meant that the affirmation was occasionally effective at alpha.

Being in control of alpha is our goal, not this hit-or-miss technique. When you are in control, you can stay at alpha as long as you need to while focusing the maximum healing energy on yourself or another person. You go to alpha with desire, belief, and expectation. You visualize the problem, imagine the health abnormality to be corrected, and then imagine the situation restored to normal. You end your alpha session.

Coué's verbalized suggestions are fine at beta. Words are the "stuff" of beta. But mental images are alpha "stuff." At beta, you are dealing with the objective, material world—the effect. At alpha, you are working in the subjective, spiritual world—the *cause* of the effect. Work mentally at alpha and you create the desired effect in the physical world. Desire, belief, and expectation, because they catalyze programming, help you to work more effectively at both the alpha and beta levels and in both the spiritual realm of causes and the physical realm of effects.

Session 11
Avoiding Opposition

1. Close your eyes and roll them slightly upward toward your eyebrows.
2. You are now ready to reduce your count from 100 to 1 to 50 to 1. Also, steps 2A, 3A, 3B, and 3C are optional. Count slowly and silently from 50 to 1. Wait about one second between numbers.
   A. Starting with your scalp, focus your conscious awareness on the parts of your body from head to toe, relaxing them as you go.
3. When you reach the count of 1, hold a picture of yourself in your mind as youthful, radiant, healthy, and attractive.
   A. Ask yourself mentally, "Why do I have this physical problem?" Then let your mind wander.
   B. When you find yourself thinking about a certain person, picture that person.
   C. Picture yourself forgiving each other. Imagine a hug or a handshake, smiles, and heads nodding in agreement. Feel good about this.
4. Repeat mentally, "I will always maintain a perfectly healthy body and mind."
5. Say to yourself, "I am going to count from 1 to 5; when I reach the count of 5, I will open my eyes, feeling fine and in perfect health, feeling better than before."
6. Count. When you reach 3, repeat, "When I reach the count of 5, I will open my eyes, feeling fine and in perfect health, feeling better than before."
7. At the count of 5, open your eyes and affirm mentally, "I am wide awake, feeling fine and in perfect health, feeling better than before. And this is so."

Physicist Eugene Wigner has said, "The very study of the external world led to the conclusion that the content of consciousness is an ultimate reality." We now know that the content of our consciousness produces our state of health, which for most of us is the ultimate reality. Without good health, we are without the joys of family, work, travel, and creature comforts. In the face of illness, these realities fade away.

Science reluctantly accepted the mind as having a role in reality, but that acceptance is finally becoming more and more widespread. Psychiatrists were probably the first physicians to take the mind seriously as a health factor. Now endocrinologists and molecular biologists are climbing aboard. At the front line of therapy, such specialists as dentists and obstetricians are also seeing the effects of the mind.

Psychoneuroimmunology now has its own quarterly journal, called *Advances*. Here, events formerly swept under the rug are now examined under the bright light of scientific scrutiny. These subjects include, for example, monkeys that, when separated from their mothers, showed a decreased ability to ward off disease but whose immune systems were strengthened when they were returned to a supportive group. Another example is the study of husbands of women dying of cancer who themselves suffered a decreased ability to ward off disease. Yet another is a person who used relaxed visual imagery to slow a tumor's growth but whose tumor's growth resumed when the exercise ceased.

The editor of *Nature* magazine, John Maddox, reports that some psychoneuroimmunologists believe that every state of mind produces a greater or lesser state of immunity (*Brain/Mind Bulletin*, Vol. 10, No. 2). The report asserts that asthmatics at the University of California, San Francisco, Medical School who took an imaginary trip through their bodies to help troubled cells needed less medication and also enjoyed improved breathing.

Opposition From the Medical Profession

The campaign to promote an understanding of the mind's role in our health has not been without its martyrs. Many physicians who have accepted the mind's role have been harassed by their local medical associations and the parent group, the American Medical Association. Medical authorities gave Dr. Carl Simonton, one of the first to adopt part of the Silva Method for patients' use, quite a hard time. Even today if you use your mind in the presence of an ill person to help that person recover you can be accused of practicing medicine without a license.

I have made an effort to protect Silva practitioners from this accusation. Picturing another person regaining health while you meditate is so close to prayer, if it is not one and the same, that I have actually formed a nonprofit corporation called the Ecumenical Society, under whose rubric people can safely enter the sick room and use healing methods. The idea had its origin back in the years between 1953 and 1963, when I was still researching the Silva Method and was experiencing my share of challenges from various authorities. One day the district attorney phoned and asked me to see him. When I arrived, his secretary ushered me into his office, where he greeted me politely and invited me to sit down. We had known each other since childhood and greeted each other by first names. But in the severe environment of a law enforcement official, niceties have a way of being blotted out.

"José," he said, "there is a complaint against you. A doctor is complaining that you healed one of his patients. He says you are practicing medicine without a license. Just what are you people doing?"

I explained that what I did was more like praying for the patient than anything else. After listening, the district attorney reassured me that the doctor had no case against me. If the patient had complained, he said, there would have been a case, but the patient was far from complaining. He was grateful for being healed.

As it turned out, I had not even been aware of this particular healing until the district attorney summoned me to his office. In this case, the doctor had prescribed a series of injections, two per week for several weeks, to correct a condition in the patient. During this time, the patient had decided to come to my Friday meetings. In the course of participating in the mental exercises I conducted at the start of each meeting, the patient's health problem cleared up. I never even knew about the problems or the cure.

The patient stopped going to the doctor, but one day he saw the doctor in town, and the doctor asked him, "Why did you stop coming for your injections?"

"Because they healed me over there," replied the patient, meaning at the Silva place. That was when the doctor complained to the district attorney.

But the district attorney himself had relatives who were attending my Friday night sessions as regulars. He ended our little meeting by advising me on how to proceed without getting into trouble. I congratulated myself at having relatives of some of our city and county officials as members of the movement and came up with the idea of the Ecumenical Society.

Opposition From the Church

The doctors were not the only ones giving Silva people a hard time. Many local church officials did so as well. Even those who knew people I had helped did not want to believe in the effectiveness of my methods until they saw them work first hand. One day a priest whom I had once helped called me. He had a friend, another priest, who had cancer of the digestive system and had already had three major operations. The sick priest had a constant fever and diarrhea. He had already been relieved of his obligation to serve and had retired to a rest home. My friend asked me to help even though local clergy were warning their congregations away from Silva meetings, suggesting that I was working for the devil. I asked my priest friend, "You mean that the priests there will allow me to come into the building to see the sick priest?"

"I will arrange it so that nobody there will bother you," he assured me.

As soon as I entered the sick priest's room, the other priests there left us alone. I felt the priest's hand, got a good impression of his face and voice, and recommended that he drink half a glass of water at night and the other half in the morning. Then I told him I would return in three days to check on his progress. At home that night I finished the programming at a distance. (I will explain this approach in detail later in the book.)

Three days later, I went back to check on the priest's progress, and he told me he felt a definite improvement. His fever had dropped and his diarrhea had stopped. He was now having normal bowel movements. Also, his attitude had changed—as had that of the other priests. Still, his healing took two more applications. Each time I arrived, the priests in attendance were more cordial.

One month later the priest went on a vacation to Spain, and when he returned he was reassigned to a church. At this writing, he is still alive.

Supposition Replaces Opposition

A generation has passed and still practitioners are meeting Silva with skepticism. But there is movement forward. In religion, instead of saying that we are "of the devil," church people and church goers are remembering what Rabbi Jesus did during His stay on earth. And they are recalling His statements about human beings' capabilities. Now they are asking, "Suppose what Jesus said is true?"

The medical profession is still beating the drums for strict allopathic approaches, but in some medical circles the question is being asked, "Suppose the mind is used in this case . . . ?"

There were days when my wife was shunned by the neighbors and my children shamed in school, but that time has passed. Laredo, Texas, is now on the map—at least partly owing to its position as the international headquarters of the Silva Mind Control Method, which has millions of graduates. Countless people, graduates and their friends and families, have benefited in every aspect of health.

With your daily morning practice, you have been building up your expectation and belief in the efficacy of the method. The more you expect and believe, the less you will stand in your own way, and the more dramatic will be your success. The late Walter Russell, codiscoverer of heavy water (which presaged the atomic age), architect, sculptor of three presidents, composer, author, and possessor of many other creative skills, was once told by an admirer, "You must have tremendous faith."

"I have no faith at all," Russell snapped back. "I *know*."

Soon you, too, will "know." You will have mastered the alpha level. You will be able to help your body and those of others to heal. From there you can go on to solving other kinds of problems.

Hundreds of physicians in all specialties have taken the Silva Method training, as have many hundreds of nurses. Leading corporations have sent their top executives to take the training and to activate more of their minds. Accountants, engineers, laborers, teachers, parents and children from all walks of life are now using the training to heighten their intuition, creativity, and problem-solving abilities.

The Silva method will help you solve many problems, but health is the easiest way to begin. Health is the top priority of the brain's neurons. When your mind programs those brain cells to act for better health, they respond readily.

Session 12
The Climate for Healing

1. Close your eyes and roll them slightly upward toward your eyebrows.
2. Steps 2A, 3A, 3B, and 3C are optional. Count slowly and silently from 50 to 1. Wait about one second between numbers.
   A. Starting with your scalp, focus your conscious awareness on the different parts of your body from head to toe, relaxing them as you go.
3. When you reach the count of 1, hold a picture of yourself in your mind as youthful, radiant, healthy, and attractive.
   A. Ask yourself mentally, "Why do I have this physical problem?" Then let your mind wander.
   B. When you find yourself thinking about a certain person, picture that person.
   C. Picture yourself forgiving each other. Imagine a hug or a handshake, smiles, and heads nodding in agreement. Feel good about this.
4. Repeat mentally, "I will always maintain a perfectly healthy body and mind."
5. Say to yourself, "I am going to count from 1 to 5; when I reach the count of 5, I will open my eyes, feeling fine and in perfect health, feeling better than before."
6. Count. When you reach 3, repeat, "When I reach the count of 5, I will open my eyes, feeling fine and in perfect health, feeling better than before."
7. At the count of 5, open your eyes and affirm mentally, "I am wide awake, feeling fine and in perfect health, feeling better than before. And this is so."

Reversing Diabetes

T.S., twenty-five, was suffering from diabetes and many of its complications when he decided to take the Silva Method training. Here, in his own words, is the result of what happened:

The main reason I participated in the Silva Method Basic Lecture Series was because of my health. I have been a Type I (insulin-dependent) diabetic for twenty years. When I reached age twenty-one, I started to develop side effects. The first side effect was diabetic retinopathy. Hemorrhages in my eyes caused me to go blind in my right eye and caused severe vision loss in my left. I had full-scale laser beam surgery in both eyes. Later I recovered some of the vision in my right eye, but it is nothing like my normal vision.

I was told by my doctors that I could no longer do any physical activity other than walking (no running, bending, lifting of any kind, etc.). This was like a bad dream to me, since all my life I had been an active athlete. All I could think was, Why me? I'm only twenty-one years old.

Later on that year I developed high blood pressure and was put on the maximum dosage of a blood pressure drug along with a diuretic. The doctors said that there was no way I could ever go off my blood pressure medication. Not only is high blood pressure bad for one's cardiovascular health, but in my condition it is a threat to the eyes.

When I turned twenty-three I was told that another complication had developed. My kidneys were going downhill. At that time I had already lost fifty percent of my kidney function.

Now I'm twenty-five and I believe that the Silva Method and God have saved my life. Since I took the course, my insulin requirements have been dropping every week. I have been programming for this to happen. I am on an insulin pump, where the dose is changed three times a day (steptype progression). I have actually programmed for the time of day for my insulin needs to drop, and it is happening! My blood pressure medication dose has also been lowered by my doctors. I have also been programming and pray-

ing for my eyes to get better, especially for the bleeding to stop. In the past just my getting mad would cause a hemorrhage.

I am now playing tennis and riding a bike, though of course very carefully. For me, the Silva Method has been more than coincidence. My doctors cannot explain the changes, but say, "Keep on doing whatever you're doing."

Can you picture T.S.? Is he a positive thinker? Yes. Is he wracked with fear, hostility, and insecurity? Hardly. Does he believe in a spiritual basis to the material world? Yes.

T.S. was motivated to take the training by the seriousness of his physical condition (desire). He believed he could program his insulin at will, and he could. He expected his programming to work and it did. In other words, he had the perfect mental climate for success. And he used it.

Overcoming Negative Thinking

Negative thinking causes problems.

Positive thinking causes solutions.

Negative thinking provides a climate in which health problems can develop.

Positive thinking provides a climate in which good health can be attained and maintained.

Let me refresh your understanding by defining each type of thinking.

Negative thinking is guilt, worry, insecurity, fear, jealousy, suspicion, hatred, antagonism, anger, despair, mourning, and self-doubt. Negative thinking is being out of step with people and things around you.

Positive thinking is love, appreciation, optimism, security, courage, cooperation, compassion, generosity, friendliness, patience, helpfulness, and ambition. Positive thinking is being in step—in harmony—with people and things around you.

These are just examples, not the whole picture. You do not

need to have the whole picture. You need only to have the picture of your own thinking, especially of any negative components. Take guilt, for example. Like any component of negative thinking, guilt is stressful. Guilt, or any other type of negative thinking, becomes habitual, and the stress it causes becomes chronic. Chronic stress is a killer.

When you feel you have not done enough, or that you have done the wrong thing, or that you have not tried hard enough, you feel guilty. If you continue to feel this way, you can be causing damage to your immune system. In the long or short run, that damage will do you in.

When you hold negative attitudes for prolonged periods, chemical changes take place in your body. A stress chemical is released into the blood, which inhibits the work of the immune system, apparently by confusing and weakening the system. In these circumstances, health problems start to build up. But positive feelings about yourself and the work you are doing, leading you to be optimistic rather than pessimistic, contribute to health. This is better for your health and, ultimately, your survival. It is also better for you to do what you know is right, so that you are not plagued by guilt feelings. It is as if nature, or God, has provided a reward system. Do right and your health thrives. Do wrong and your health suffers.

Any time you feel pangs of conscience about what you are doing, stop. Go to your alpha level. Identify the action that is giving you the guilt feelings. Resolve to undo this action and not to repeat it. From 1 to 5, open your eyes, and notice how much better you feel.

Even the thought of doing something that is not totally fair, considerate, moral, legal, or correct can be stressful. The temptation alone can make you sick.

Whenever a wrongful thought enters your mind, stop. Close your eyes, take a deep breath, turn your eyes slightly upward, and mentally say, "Cancel, cancel." You will have diffused that source of stress on the spot. This is good practice at the onset of any negative thought.

Session 13
The Need for Faith

1. Close your eyes and roll them slightly upward toward your eyebrows.
2. Steps 2A, 3A, 3B, and 3C are optional. Count slowly and silently from 50 to 1. Wait about one second between numbers.
   A. Starting with your scalp, focus your conscious awareness on the different parts of your body from head to toe, relaxing them as you go.
3. When you reach the count of 1, hold a picture of yourself in your mind as youthful, radiant, healthy, and attractive.
   A. Ask yourself mentally, "Why do I have this physical problem?" Then let your mind wander.
   B. When you find yourself thinking about a certain person, picture that person.
   C. Picture yourself forgiving each other. Imagine a hug or a handshake, smiles, and heads nodding in agreement. Feel good about this.
4. Repeat mentally, "I will always maintain a perfectly healthy body and mind."
5. Say to yourself, "I am going to count from 1 to 5; when I reach the count of 5, I will open my eyes, feeling fine and in perfect health, feeling better than before."
6. Count. When you reach 3, repeat, "When I reach the count of 5, I will open my eyes, feeling fine and in perfect health, feeling better than before."
7. At the count of 5, open your eyes and affirm mentally, "I am wide awake, feeling fine and in perfect health, feeling better than before. And this is so."

The Many Paths to Illness

No one can say for sure which specific mental attitudes or emotions cause such illnesses as multiple sclerosis, diabetes, and the Guillain-Barré Syndrome. These diseases are not easily attributable to specific attitudes or emotions, whereas it is often quite clear that a woman may lose her hearing because there is something she does not want to hear or a man may lose his eyesight because there is something he does not want to see.

There are many paths by which illness can arrive. It can come by way of heredity, for example; it can ride the air we breathe or the water we drink. It can be in food additives or environmental pollutants. It can result from a shortage of sleep, exercise, nutrients, or vitamins, and from many other causes.

Some feel that illness appears to teach a lesson; they see illness as a blessing in disguise. I do not agree. Our Creator wants us to be perfect, as He is. Deviations from that perfection are made not in heaven but on earth.

People cause their own health problems. I firmly believe this. Sister Elizabeth Reis, a Silva lecturer, believes differently. She has her reasons. I'll let her explain in her own words:

Guillain-Barré Syndrome: A strange, unique experience; a little-known "disease" until it enters your life.

Where does it come from?

How does it affect people?

What can one do with it through prayer, Silva Method techniques, positive attitudes, fearlessness, faith, or inner trust?

On August 23 I was invited to St. Mary Convent, Port Huron, Michigan, to begin my book Biblical Reflections, *a manuscript coming out of twenty-five years of teaching scripture internationally.*

Chapters 1 and 2 were complete. Now a question arose. "Where do I go next? Biblical truth or universal truth?" There was much involved in this question, since, as a Christian and a Silva Mind Control Method lecturer, I had often been both challenged and attacked: "How does the Silva Method fit into the message of Jesus?"

We prayed on Wednesday, August 25, for an answer to that question. Thursday I woke up with double vision. At eleven a.m. I couldn't walk. By midnight I was totally paralyzed. An answer to prayer? "Ask, and one always receives; seek and one always finds."

I went to the emergency room at Mercy Hospital, Port Huron. By ten that evening I had had a brain scan, a CAT scan, and several diagnoses. Eventually the tests pointed to Guillain-Barré Syndrome, a disease caused by a virus that affects the neurological system through the spinal column.

Every muscle in my body had stopped, beginning with my eyes. Interesting symbol—a movement toward clarity in inner vision, perhaps?

Six Sisters of Joseph and friends from all over Michigan arrived to be a twenty-four-hour nursing/prayer crew . . . six people of love, prayer, and faith, Silva graduates (all but one) and long-time friends.

I was carried by their energy and presence. Never was I afraid. Never was I in pain. Through years of both prayer and Silva Method training, I had long ago learned how to relax, so my blood pressure, temperature, and pulse were normal throughout the experience. I didn't "work at it." This was a daily event that had already been established by practice, practice, practice.

Once a nurse took my blood pressure and found it was low. I said, "Give me a moment and take it again." She did—and: "Normal!"

The throat muscles didn't work, so there was a possibility of the lungs being affected. My twenty-four-hour friends gargled me around the clock, so that, too, was avoided. I was suctioned but never placed on a respirator. Again, all very unique for the kind of pattern Guillain-Barré Syndrome seems to follow. Guillain-Barré Syndrome seems to take six months to several years for recovery. But within thirty days I was released by my delighted and amazed doctor . . . walking, talking, flying: a sign of the effectiveness of what José Silva calls energy, visualization, relaxation; what a Christian/holy person calls the prayer of faith.

I now call this marvelous experience of learning and healing my "thirty-day retreat."

I was totally paralyzed for ten days . . . waiting for the eyes to begin movement. We then went by ambulance to Borgess, our hospital in Kalamazoo, and again for exactly ten days I had physical therapy.

We arrived at Borgess on Sunday afternoon, September 5. Monday morning therapy began; by evening I was moving my arms and standing. Again, when one knows the history of others with this virus disease, you appreciate the power of relaxation, energy, and prayer.

As the medical personnel at Borgess watched my amazing recovery, I prepared to return to Nazareth and our medical floor at Fontbonne (our retired sisters building).

Again the "magic ten days" of love and care along with daily physical therapy has now brought me to a point of physical independence. My eyes are not quite together in their movement. I feel like the man in the gospel who saw "men like trees walking." I'm fine with that, and with a little patience. . . .

My question now is, "What have I learned and how can I share it with the universe?" Certainly, my book will never be the same, nor will I.

It was not "laid on me" by God. It was not satanic. I asked to understand physical pain. I had already suffered emotionally, spiritually, and mentally. And because of this, counseling was not difficult in these areas. But physically? I was always healthy, so I was often arrogant with the physically weak. I now praise God for this particular experience. It has allowed me to recognize that everyone is learning.

Healing is not an accident; it is a natural flow, which, when allowed to function, truly, "does its thing." It is also a universal flow that can be assisted by the prayer and thoughts of others.

Perhaps this story may remind us that none of us is alone. We are our "brother's keeper"; we are our brother.

Your energy is mine because we all draw from the same source! It is a gift and it is real.

I call it God, and as a Christian, I recognize the "good news."

The Many Paths to Wellness

Sister Elizabeth Reis's experience is an inspiration to many, as she continues to share it with classes and audiences wherever she teaches and lectures.

One's faith in God is a factor in healing and wellness. The more alone we feel, the more stress we experience. Any religion that acknowledges a Higher Intelligence is stress relieving. For the same reason, the love of family is a path to wellness.

Session 14
Gaining Peace of Mind

1. Close your eyes and roll them slightly upward toward your eyebrows.
2. Steps 2A, 3A, 3B, and 3C are optional. Count slowly and silently from 50 to 1. Wait about one second between numbers.
   A. Starting with your scalp, focus your conscious awareness on the different parts of your body from head to toe, relaxing them as you go.
3. When you reach the count of 1, hold a picture of yourself in your mind as youthful, radiant, healthy, and attractive.
   A. Ask yourself mentally, "Why do I have this physical problem?" Then let your mind wander.
   B. When you find yourself thinking about a certain person, picture that person.
   C. Picture yourself forgiving each other. Imagine a hug or a handshake, smiles, and heads nodding in agreement. Feel good about this.
4. Repeat mentally, "I will always maintain a perfectly healthy body and mind."
5. Say to yourself, "I am going to count from 1 to 5; when I reach the count of 5, I will open my eyes, feeling fine and in perfect health, feeling better than before."
6. Count. When you reach 3, repeat, "When I reach the count of 5, I will open my eyes, feeling fine and in perfect health, feeling better than before."
7. At the count of 5, open your eyes and affirm mentally, "I am wide awake, feeling fine and in perfect health, feeling better than before. And this is so."

The awareness of our ability to make ourselves sick or well is growing. For example, it used to be unthinkable to see cancer research along any but medical-chemical lines. However, in late 1984 the American Cancer Research Fund issued a survey on stress and its relation to cancer. "We have launched this effort in the area of stress-related cancer because many studies show a strong link between levels of stress and chances of getting cancer," says the transmittal letter. The letter cites these three specific studies:

1. Dr. William H. Green of the University of Rochester studied the lives of three sets of twins. One twin out of each set experienced psychological upheaval and shortly afterwards developed leukemia (cancer of the blood), while the stress-free twin did not.
2. Dr. H. J. F. Baltrush reported to the Third International Symposium on Detection and Prevention of Cancer that, after studying eight thousand patients with different types of cancers, he determined that in the majority of cases, cancer came on "during a period of severe and intensive life stress frequently involving loss, separation, and other bereavements."
3. Independent studies by Dr. Caroline B. Thomas of Johns Hopkins and Dr. René C. Mastrovito from Memorial Sloan Kettering Cancer Center showed the highest incidence of cancer among people who tended to keep their emotions "bottled up."

It is good news to see an awareness of the human mind's potential to cause either illness or health filtering into the consciousness of the medical profession. But the slow rate of progress is frustrating to those of us who are already experiencing the positive results that flow from this understanding.

It is good news to see educators opening their minds to the importance of right-brain functioning, but here too the progress is frustratingly slow.

More and more people from widely diverse backgrounds are recognizing the value of the enhanced creativity, perception, and intuition that comes with alpha control.

May the movement accelerate and its numbers increase.

How to Lower Stress and Gain Peace of Mind

N.B. was being driven to work by her husband when the car ahead stopped suddenly. She was eating a bowl of cornflakes at the time. "My head bumped into the dashboard. My lips pushed into the cereal bowl. My breakfast flew everywhere—into my hair, my handbag, over my pretty floral dress. . . ."

There was no damage to the car, but the couple had to turn around and go home to get cleaned up. N.B. called the office to report the delay. She was visibly shaken up and mentally unnerved. She used the Silva Method to go to her alpha level. Quickly she undid negative emotions and substituted positive in their place: "I am thankful I am not hurt. Only good will come of this, because that is what I seek. I am going to have a great day. My husband is going to have a great day. My nerves are calming down. I feel more and more peaceful. When I open my eyes at the count of 5, I will feel wonderful."

When she counted herself out, she felt an immediate difference. "My husband witnessed a different me. He did not have to carry my bag or help me in any way. Instead of bemoaning the event, I was putting it behind me. He was proud of me."

To dispel the stress of the moment, do what N.B. did. Go to your alpha level and turn the situation around. Picture the glass of your life not as half empty but as half full. Give yourself mental instructions to profit from the experience. Program yourself to restore your mental equilibrium and to use the experience to become an even better self than you were before.

Make a habit of dispelling stress and substituting peace of mind. Go over yesterday's activities and pinpoint any stressful event, searching especially for some action in which you were less than generous, ethical, legally fair, or compassionate toward someone else. At your alpha level, resolve to do something today to rectify that action. Or, if you took no action instead of helping somebody, resolve to take some positive action today. At night, do the same thing for the day just ended. Doing this regularly produces a peaceful state of mind, which is a prerequisite to longevity.

Biofeedback and Stress Control

Biofeedback equipment measures internal physical states. Because these states are indicative of mental states, biofeedback has become a popular way of making changes in mental states and confirming that those changes have indeed taken place. With biofeedback, for instance, you can confirm that you are at the correct level of relaxation to dispel stress.

A thermometer is a biofeedback device. It does not measure level of relaxation, but it does provide valuable information about body temperature. Relaxation is measurable by two biofeedback devices. One measures the electrical resistance of the skin. The other measures brain frequencies.

I make both instruments available to Silva Method students. They can obtain a galvanic skin reactor to help in their relaxation practice. By placing two fingers on the electrode pads, turning on the instruments, and adjusting the audio pulsations to a point midway between slow and fast, students can relax and obtain immediate audio feedback regarding their successes. Although the galvanic skin reactor does not measure brain-wave frequency and gives information about relaxation that is more qualitative than quantitative, I have calibrated it so that the audio beeps are at their slowest point when a person is deeply relaxed.

An electroencephalograph is necessary to get a true measure of alpha. This is a more elaborate and therefore more expensive biofeedback device than the galvanic skin reactor. Within the electroencephalograph, electrodes are attached directly to the head of the user, and either a visual (dial) or audio feedback is used to indicate when the alpha frequencies have been reached.

Using either device, students can learn whether the techniques they are using are really relaxing the body and mind. In counting down, they can determine whether it is more effective to picture the numbers or to mentally state the numbers. They can determine which peaceful scene is most effective: that beautiful lake or a swing in the backyard. And they can determine which is the best method for their progressive relaxation. Are they better off simply ordering their shoulders to relax or actually moving them around to find a relaxed position? These kinds of questions are quickly answered by the rate of beeps they hear or by the dial they see. In this way, users learn exactly what relaxes them.

Perhaps an even more important value of these biofeedback devices is their ability to convince students that something is indeed happening when they relax by counting backwards. With this assurance, students become more relaxed about relaxation. If you are "uptight" about whether you are really relaxed, you are, of course, not relaxed. By assuring students of relaxation that they are actually progressing, biofeedback is contributing to that progress.

Contributing to relaxation is contributing to stress management—but not to the elimination of stress. Biofeedback's limitation is that, while it can help you handle or dispel stress, it cannot help you prevent stress from developing. For this you need to use your alpha level to make decisions and corrections, as described above.

Session 15
Diffusing Destructive Thoughts

1. Close your eyes and roll them slightly upward toward your eyebrows.
2. Steps 2A, 3A, 3B, and 3C are optional. Count slowly and silently from 50 to 1. Wait about one second between numbers.
   A. Starting with your scalp, focus your conscious awareness on the different parts of your body from head to toe, relaxing them as you go.
3. When you reach the count of 1, hold a picture of yourself in your mind as youthful, radiant, healthy, and attractive.
   A. Ask yourself mentally, "Why do I have this physical problem?" Then let your mind wander.
   B. When you find yourself thinking about a certain person, picture that person.
   C. Picture yourself forgiving each other. Imagine a hug or a handshake, smiles, and heads nodding in agreement. Feel good about this.
4. Repeat mentally, "I will always maintain a perfectly healthy body and mind."
5. Say to yourself, "I am going to count from 1 to 5; when I reach the count of 5, I will open my eyes, feeling fine and in perfect health, feeling better than before."
6. Count. When you reach 3, repeat, "When I reach the count of 5, I will open my eyes, feeling fine and in perfect health, feeling better than before."
7. At the count of 5, open your eyes and affirm mentally, "I am wide awake, feeling fine and in perfect health, feeling better than before. And this is so."

Acute depression in people has been found to result in a high susceptibility to cancer and viral infections such as herpes. When the depression ends, the immune system is freed to perform normally, and these risks appear to subside.

The mechanics of just how this works is currently the subject of research by biochemists and immunologists. These researchers are able to detect chain reactions that trace the brain-immune system connection. We in the Silva Method do not take part in this research. Nor do we sit idly by. On the assumption that everything in the body is coordinated by the mind, we go about controlling the mind in order to control the immune system, the vital organs, and our general levels of good health.

Yes, you can fight disease by controlling your moods. While scientists look for the pathways that link the brain with the body's line of defense, you do not have to wait for their discoveries. You can use your alpha level to move your moods toward the positive side of the mood spectrum—and live longer.

It is my philosophy that we are rewarded by our Creator for helping to correct the problems of creation. We are here to help God with this manifest world. We are the only creatures in the world who can act as co-creators. We alone are able to make this a better world to live in, both for humans and other forms of life. As we work in this direction, life gets better for us, too. As each of us thinks creatively rather than destructively, positively rather than negatively, we ourselves are the first to benefit by living healthier and longer lives.

On the other hand, if we think destructively, if we are depressed, if we "put others down," we are the first to suffer from our opposition to creation. We lose our immunity to disease and succumb to tiny germs and viruses. Talk about the punishment fitting the crime! If we think destructively, we destroy ourselves.

The "Punishment" to Fit the "Crime"

The nature of destructive thoughts is frequently made clear in the nature of the damage they do to our body. The thought picks the words, and the words order the body to comply. But words can be bypassed, and indeed most of our thoughts are nonverbal.

Continuous friction, such as a pipe on the lips of an inveterate smoker, can cause cancer. But cancer has been known to be caused by human friction, too—by an overbearing supervisor, for example, or an "impossible" mother-in-law. And allowing oneself to be consumed by the desire for something unattainable has been known to cause consumption or tuberculosis.

On a more physiologically localized level, secret frustrations can appear on the skin in the form of psoriasis. Frustrations over one's progress has been known to cause knee or foot problems. Business worries or chronic anxiety can hit you in the "gut"—in the form of ulcers.

Happiness Can Cure You!

Usually it is not difficult to see the connection between negative attitudes and emotions and their negative physical effects. Going on the premise that the "punishment"—or illness—fits the "crime"—or negative thoughts—you can derive important clues about what thoughts are causing your physical problem. This approach is particularly helpful for beginners. Later, as you master the alpha level, you will be able to identify these thoughts more directly, not only in yourself but also in others, as later chapters will explain.

Listening to harmonious music can be a path to wellness. Joy and laughter can be a path to wellness. Many therapists now conduct "laughter seminars" for the seriously ill. Ever since Norman Cousins, then editor of the *Saturday Review*, cured himself of what the doctors called an incurable disease by leaving the hospital and checking into a hotel with comic books, laugh records, and other laughter-inducing entertainments, the medical profession has been taking a closer look at laughter as "medicine." I could list other paths to wellness, but like those named above—

faith, love, harmony, and fun—they would all be mind-related. If the common denominator is mind and if you are able to go to the alpha level and control your mind, what else could possibly be needed?

Review of Additional Health Procedures

Here are the main procedures for enjoying a "climate" for better health:

Dealing with temptation or other negativity. Stop. Close your eyes, and turn them slightly upward. Take a deep breath. Mentally say, "Cancel, cancel." Open your eyes.

Ending a negative activity. Whenever you are involved in an activity that engenders a conflict within you, stop. Go to your alpha level. Identify the questionable activity. Resolve to undo it and not redo it. Count yourself out.

Diffusing daily stress. Upon going to bed, go to your alpha level. Go over the day's activities. Was there anything you did that was not totally considerate or ethical, anything about which you might be harboring guilt feelings? Affirm to yourself that you will do something tomorrow to rectify that act. Similarly, if there was an action you did not take that you should have taken, resolve to take that action tomorrow. Fall asleep. In the morning, repeat, and count yourself out.

Helping yourself to heal. Go to alpha. Go inside your body in your imagination to where the problem is. Imagine you are fixing yourself. Picture perfect health. Count yourself out, affirming your wellness.

Session 16
Pain and Hypnosis

1. Close your eyes and roll them slightly upward toward your eyebrows.
2. Steps 2A, 3A, 3B, and 3C are optional. Count slowly and silently from 50 to 1. Wait about one second between numbers.
   A. Starting with your scalp, focus your conscious awareness on the different parts of your body from head to toe, relaxing them as you go.
3. When you reach the count of 1, hold a picture of yourself in your mind as youthful, radiant, healthy, and attractive.
   A. Ask yourself mentally, "Why do I have this physical problem?" Then let your mind wander.
   B. When you find yourself thinking about a certain person, picture that person.
   C. Picture yourself forgiving each other. Imagine a hug or a handshake, smiles, and heads nodding in agreement. Feel good about this.
4. Repeat mentally, "I will always maintain a perfectly healthy body and mind."
5. Say to yourself, "I am going to count from 1 to 5; when I reach the count of 5, I will open my eyes, feeling fine and in perfect health, feeling better than before."
6. Count. When you reach 3, repeat, "When I reach the count of 5, I will open my eyes, feeling fine and in perfect health, feeling better than before."
7. At the count of 5, open your eyes and affirm mentally, "I am wide awake, feeling fine and in perfect health, feeling better than before. And this is so."

The relief of pain, the inhibition of excessive bleeding, the acceleration of the healing process—these are all steps that you can take when you know how to go to the alpha level and use it in a controlled way.

Did you know that a person can affect the ability of bacteria to survive or succumb to a poison?

Did you know that a person can stop pain dead in its tracks even if it is a chronic pain that has caused suffering for years?

Did you know that a person can help another person at a distance to relieve suffering and recover from an injury?

These are the types of capabilities you are now developing as you gain control of the alpha level of the mind, and these are the capabilities we will activate in this chapter. As we proceed together in the chapters ahead, you will find the capabilities becoming awe-inspiring. The mind can make us sick and the mind can keep us well. And this is so.

Hypnosis and Mesmerism

Today we take for granted the many over-the-counter and prescription drugs available to control pain. But in the early 1800s, no such drugs existed. Major surgery was conducted with a bottle of whiskey and four strong men. The patient drank the whiskey, the men positioned themselves at each arm and leg to hold the patient down, and the surgeon cut.

It was shortly after that time that a British doctor named Esdaile took a team of mesmerizers to India to conduct a series of tests using Mesmer's energy principles. Dr. Esdaile demonstrated in India that when mesmerizers made passes over a subject's body from head to foot, keeping the hands about three inches away from the body, the subject would become anesthetized. The doctor was able to perform major surgery, such as amputations, without four strong men and a bottle of whiskey and without introducing any chemical anesthetic into the body.

A side effect of these mesmeric passes that Dr. Esdaile discovered was an antiseptic bonus. Sterilization appeared to result from the passes. The incidence of infection dropped to less than 5 percent as compared with other methods. I have investigated this process and have found that the mesmerizer's brain frequency slows while making the passes. The energy transmitted by the hands of the mesmerizer, whose brain is functioning at the alpha level, penetrates the subject's body and appears to stimulate and excite subatomic particles in matter, causing the numbness.

I have seen a number of operations performed by healers using this method. In one such operation, a tumor was removed from the arm of a patient without the use of chemical anesthesia. There was no pain and, even though the surgical instrument was not sterilized, there was no bleeding and no infection.

Mesmerism had much in common with hypnosis. In my study and practice of hypnosis over the years, I have found that hypnosis in a waking state can be used quite effectively as an anesthetic. The first recorded use of hypnosis in surgery also took place in India. After observing fakirs lying on beds of nails painlessly, a British doctor developed a hypnosis-inducing technique that he used successfully on his patients. When he demonstrated the technique to a committee of doctors, they walked away and submitted a report saying that there was no such thing as hypnosis and that these surgical patients were just doing what the doctor asked them to do. It seems they would do anything but accept the reality!

Hypnosis, the Brain's Special Pain Reliever

Hypnotism is a perfect anesthetic. It can be used to anesthetize any part of the body without the allergic or side effects that chemical anesthetics frequently cause. You can even draw a circle with your finger on some part of the patient's body and create a numbness within that circle only.

Hypnotism creates numbness via the brain. The hypnotist's words act as "commands" to the brain. The brain complies by creating a numbness in the specified area. It does so by sending to the area its own natural chemical anesthetic, chemicals called endorphins, which stop pain and create a feeling of euphoria.

In the thirty-two-hour Silva Method training, about one-half hour is devoted to a session in which students use a hypnotic technique to create numbness in one hand (left hand for the right-handed). They image this hand to be immersed in an imaginary bucket of ice-cold water. After a few minutes of sitting with their hands dangling in this imaginary bucket, they place their hands back on their laps and test them by pinching them. Most students are able to create a decided numbness the first time. Those who are able to detect only small changes are asked to practice this procedure to improve their results. Once the hand is numb, they find they can then place it over a painful area of the body and mentally transfer the numbness to that point. This mental transfer takes place physically. Endorphins appear in the brain and the pain disappears.

In your work with this book so far, you have trained yourself in deep relaxation and realistic imagining. You are already able to use self-direction in obtaining a numbness in your hand as just described. Here are the steps:

1. Sit in a straight-backed chair, close your eyes, turn them slightly upward, and count backward to reach alpha.
2. Deepen your relaxation by doing more counting backward; I recommend counting backward from 100 to 1.
3. Lower your least strong hand (left if you are right-handed) to the side of your chair into an imaginary bucket of ice-cold water. Feel the pieces of ice; recall a time when you actually had your hand in a bucket of ice water.
4. Keep your hand in the imaginary bucket of ice water for five minutes, knowing that your hand is getting colder and colder, more and more numb.
5. Take your hand out of the imaginary bucket and test it for numbness by pinching it with your other hand.

6. Restore all feeling by rubbing your numb hand from the wrist out several times, mentally saying "Hand normal."
7. Remind yourself that you can create such numbness again merely by remembering this event, and that you can transfer this numbness to your other hand or to any painful part of your body by merely placing your numb hand over that part.
8. Count yourself out, feeling great.

A Beta Way to End Pain

Theta brain frequencies are involved with hypnotism, so the standard Silva Method first-aid treatment is an adaptation of the hypnotic technique just described to reach the theta level.

However, there is another way to end pain without going to the alpha or theta level. It is most successful for chronic pain and for pain that has existed for some time.

Pain is nature's way of saying that something needs your attention. The hand-numbing procedure above is a first-aid procedure. It is to be used to relieve pain until you can have the pained area checked by a health care specialist. Or use this method when drugs are recommended.

But when the pain has been checked, all necessary tests and treatments are completed, and you still have the pain, use this beta procedure:

1. Point to the exact location of the pain.
2. If the pain could fit a container, what container size would be perfect for it (can, bottle, box, etc.)?
3. If the pain had a color, what color would it be? Feel the pain. What color is it?
4. If the pain had a taste, what would it taste like? Feel the pain. How does it taste?
5. If the pain had a smell, what would it smell like? Feel the pain. How does it smell?
6. Go through Steps 1 to 5 again, noticing changes in the location, shape, color, taste, and smell.

7. If there is still some pain left, repeat the cycles (Steps 1 through 5) a few more times if necessary, until you can no longer locate or feel the pain.

Mrs. L.W. had bursitis for five years. After going through the above cycle four times, she could no longer find any pain, no matter how she moved her shoulder. Weeks later, the pain had not returned.

Mr. R.B. had an attack of gout in his big toe one morning. Gout is said to be one of the most intense of pains. Sufferers liken it to having the toe in a vise, tightened and then given one more turn. R.B. limped to a seminar where the above-described method was demonstrated. He volunteered to be the subject and limped to the front of the room. In five minutes, R.B. walked back to his seat free of pain and limp.

Mr. A.R. had chronic lower back pain. He conscientiously went through the cycle twice. On being asked to locate the pain to begin the third cycle, he exclaimed, "It's gone!"

Dr. C.D., a physician attending such a demonstration, volunteered to be a subject because of a painful tennis elbow. After several cycles, he could not find the pain. He refused to leave the front of the room and return to his seat. "I don't believe this," he muttered, moving his elbow around and trying to find a painful position. Eventually he returned to his seat, shaking his head in disbelief.

There is no magic to it. Pain is subjective feeling, a right-brain function. When you make an *object* out of it—giving it location, shape, color, taste, and smell—it becomes objective. Your brain obliges by sending endorphins to relieve the pain.

Some pain is with us for so long that we become possessive. We call it "my pain." To hold onto it better, we give it a specific handle: "my arthritis pain."

Chronic pain is a habit. Why suffer? Get rid of the expectation and belief that you must have it.

Break the habit. If you have a pain, do the cycle now.

Session 17
Dealing With Emergencies

1. Close your eyes and roll them slightly upward toward your eyebrows.
2. Steps 2A, 3A, 3B, and 3C are optional. Count slowly and silently from 50 to 1. Wait about one second between numbers.
   A. Starting with your scalp, focus your conscious attention on the different parts of your body from head to toe, relaxing them as you go.
3. When you reach the count of 1, hold a picture of yourself in your mind as youthful, radiant, healthy, and attractive.
   A. Ask yourself mentally, "Why do I have this physical problem?" Then let your mind wander.
   B. When you find yourself thinking about a certain person, picture that person.
   C. Picture yourself forgiving each other. Imagine a hug or a handshake, smiles, and heads nodding in agreement. Feel good about this.
4. Repeat mentally, "I will always maintain a perfectly healthy body and mind."
5. Say to yourself, "I am going to count from 1 to 5; when I reach the count of 5, I will open my eyes, feeling fine and in perfect health, feeling better than before."
6. Count. When you reach 3, repeat, "When I reach the count of 5, I will open my eyes, feeling fine and in perfect health, feeling better than before."
7. At the count of 5, open your eyes and affirm mentally, "I am wide awake, feeling fine and in perfect health, feeling better than before. And this is so."

Using Alpha in an Emergency

David Pelby, of the Winnipeg area of Canada, had an emergency of the kind nobody wants. He had taken the Silva Method training two years previously and had used it successfully for minor things in everyday life. But in March 1980, he had a major problem. Here is his own description of what happened:

I was working on a drilling rig near Wollaston Lake, Saskatchewan, Canada. I had been working about twenty feet up in the drilling tower, when I was instructed to go to the outside of the tower and wait while a certain drilling operation was made.

I was hanging onto the frame of the tower when the internal section of the drill was being lowered. I had not realized that my fingers were in the way, and before I knew it I had lost the top half of the fingers on my left hand.

Thoughts like "Stay calm, hang on" and "Don't hurt" came to mind simultaneously. I got myself together and climbed down the ladder, saying to myself, "Don't hurt, no pain, don't bleed." When I was on the ground and was able to, I applied the Silva pain technique physically. I don't know how much pain there could have been, but I do know that I have felt more pain and lost nearly as much blood from minor cuts and a bumped knee. I went to level and programmed, "No hurt, no pain, it's healed now," over and over to myself.

The next eight hours were to be more aggravating than thoughts of the accident. It took about an hour to get the bush plane warmed up and ready for takeoff. Approximately one and a half hours later I was dropped off at a makeshift airport in Lynn Lake, Manitoba. There was supposed to be an ambulance waiting for me, but it looked like I would have to wait another hour, so I gave up waiting and found my own ride to the hospital. When I got to the hospital, I asked where the ambulance had been and was told they had been misinformed as to the severity of the accident and hadn't realized it was serious enough for an ambulance.

I had to wait another hour and a half for a doctor to come to the hospital, only to be told that he couldn't do anything for me. I was informed that I would have to go to Winnipeg, which was about six hundred miles south. I had visions of getting there the following day. I then programmed that I would get the best possible service and get to Winnipeg as soon as possible. At this time, I also programmed that I would get the best doctor possible.

Within an hour, the doctor had a Lear Jet from Winnipeg in Lynn Lake, and I was immediately boarded on the jet along with a nurse. Six hundred miles and eight hours after the accident, I was in surgery in the Health Sciences Centre in Winnipeg, Manitoba, Canada.

Throughout the whole trip, I was not allowed to have anything for pain control, nor was I allowed to have any food. Throughout the entire trip, I remained fairly calm and talkative. I tried to be as cheerful as I could be, under the circumstances.

After the surgery, with good healing thoughts, the best diet possible in a very large hospital, the tender loving care and the healthy attitude of the staff in Ward H, I improved quickly. In fact, four days later I had approximately 80 to 90 percent healing of the flesh and skin on the tips of my fingers. On the fourth day, the doctor removed the stitches and commented that this was one of the finest examples of simple plastic surgery he had ever seen. One of the nurses commented that I was lucky that I had had the best doctor for my type of medical problem.

I remained in the hospital for another week for physiotherapy and was released. Three weeks after the accident, I was able to perform major tasks like turning door knobs and buttoning my clothes, for which I was grateful. Very soon I was back to work on a different job. I learned that with a healthy mind, healthy thoughts, and a healthy body, a person can produce fantastic results.

David Pelby had been using the Silva Method for two years. You might say he was a skilled alpha operator.

The Three-Fingers Technique to Activate More of the Mind

When you reach alpha, more of your mind is working for you, because the right-brain hemisphere has become activated. But even a countdown of 5 to 1 can be difficult if pain is excruciating, blood is spurting, or pandemonium is surrounding you after an accident. You need to make preparations to enable you to go to alpha in an easier way and to trigger more of your mind to go to work for you when it is needed in an emergency.

One such preparation is the Three-Fingers Technique. This involves putting your thumb and first two fingers of either hand together as a signal to the neurons in both brain hemispheres that full teamwork is needed. From the time you program this technique onward, the thumb and first two fingers of either hand are used as the trigger for alpha in health matters. When you program the Three-Fingers Technique to work for you, you can use it to help you function at a higher level of intelligence whenever the "chips are down." Use these steps to program the technique:

1. Close your eyes, turn them slightly upward, and count yourself into alpha.
2. Put your thumb and first two fingers of either hand together and repeat mentally, "Whenever I put these three fingers of either hand together, my mind works at a deeper level of awareness to normalize any injury."
3. Count yourself out and open your eyes, feeling great.

Preprogramming for Any Emergency

This programming can be extended to give you comprehensive recovery powers in any emergency.

Doing so involves the use of the Three-Fingers Technique plus one other new principle. This new principle has to do with choosing the optimum time to program yourself. Obviously, the best time to program yourself is not while you're crossing a busy intersection. Your brain-wave frequency is at high beta at such a time. Rather, the best time to program yourself is when your brain waves are already at a slower frequency. This occurs at night.

But when during the night? You can leave it up to your brain to decide. Before falling asleep, you will program yourself to awaken automatically during the night at the optimum time for programming yourself. Then, the first time you wake up during the night, you will go to your alpha level and follow the prescribed procedure. You will be at deep alpha and the programming will be decidedly effective.

If you are now ready to preprogram yourself to handle any health emergency that should arise, here is the procedure:

1. Go to your alpha level just before falling asleep.
2. At alpha, give yourself instructions to awaken automatically at the best time to program yourself for emergencies.
3. Go to sleep from alpha.
4. When you awaken during the night, again go to alpha.
5. At alpha, put the tips of your thumb and two fingers of either hand together.
6. Then tell yourself, "Whenever in the future I meet up with an emergency, all I need to do is defocus my vision. By simply gazing without focusing my eyes, I will enter the alpha level. Thus, I will be using more of my mind to come out of any emergency in the best of health."
7. Go back to sleep from alpha.

This preprogramming will allow you to go to alpha instantly no matter what the external conditions and to program for healing and health. No lengthy counting backward will be necessary. By merely staring off into space, you will be at alpha.

Session 18
First-Aid Procedures

1. Close your eyes and roll them slightly upward toward your eyebrows.
2. Steps 2A, 3A, 3B, and 3C are optional. Count slowly and silently from 50 to 1. Wait about one second between numbers.
   A. Starting with your scalp, focus your conscious awareness on the different parts of your body from head to toe, relaxing them as you go.
3. When you reach the count of 1, hold a picture of yourself in your mind as youthful, radiant, healthy, and attractive.
   A. Ask yourself mentally, "Why do I have this physical problem?" Then let your mind wander.
   B. When you find yourself thinking about a certain person, picture that person.
   C. Picture yourself forgiving each other. Imagine a hug or a handshake, smiles, and heads nodding in agreement. Feel good about this.
4. Repeat mentally, "I will always maintain a perfectly healthy body and mind."
5. Say to yourself, "I am going to count from 1 to 5; when I reach the count of 5, I will open my eyes, feeling fine and in perfect health, feeling better than before."
6. Count. When you reach 3, repeat, "When I reach the count of 5, I will open my eyes, feeling fine and in perfect health, feeling better than before."
7. At the count of 5, open your eyes and affirm mentally, "I am wide awake, feeling fine and in perfect health, feeling better than before. And this is so."

At this point, I want to introduce a new concept related to visualizing. It has to do with positioning your mental picture. When you visualize directly in front of you, you are programming in the present. When the picture you visualize is off to your right, you go into the past. When your picture is off to the left, you go into the future. Imagine yourself as facing south in your visualization. The setting sun—the past—is then to your right, and the rising sun—the future—is to your left.

When I was first researching the Silva Method, I tested it on my own children. To have them program themselves for the future—say, for better marks at school—I had them turn slightly to the left. This corresponded to the movements often seen in hypnotized subjects: they lean to the right when they regress into the past. Sometimes they lean so far to the right that it is necessary to reposition them lest they fall off their chairs.

When we program for an accelerated healing following an injury, we first visualize the situation in the present—straight ahead. Then, in an important step, we move the picture to the left slightly for twelve minutes and imagine the healing taking place. Finally, we move the picture farther to the left and imagine ourselves perfectly healed and back to normal.

Here is the healing procedure to follow after an accident. It is to take a total of fifteen minutes.

1. Defocus your eyes and enter your alpha level.
2. Visualize yourself directly in front of you, as if you were looking at yourself in a full-length mirror.
3. Take two minutes to analyze the problem, identifying the areas of greatest need.
4. Move the picture of yourself slightly to the left.
5. Imagine yourself getting better. See all the injured areas beginning to heal. Do this for twelve minutes.
6. Move the picture of yourself still further to the left.
7. Imagine yourself totally healed. For one minute, hold this picture of yourself as completely normal and healthy.
8. End your session by counting out.

Repeat this fifteen-minute session three times a day, morning, noon, and night.

Let your picture fit the injury. For instance, if the accident involves a serious burn that requires a skin graft, imagine the new skin on the burned area, imagine the liquid excretion from the area, and imagine your blood vessels joining with those of the grafted skin.

How to Halt Profuse Bleeding

If there is an accident involving lacerations that bleed, a certain amount of bleeding is necessary for the cleansing of the wound. But if the bleeding does not stop, it could be imperative that you know how to use your mind to stop it.

There have been cases in hospital surgery where, despite all the efforts of the surgery staff, hemorrhaging was not stopped. Frequently, in such cases hypnotists have been called in. Hypnotists have been known to command patients to stop bleeding even when those patients have been under general anesthesia. Much to the amazement of the surgeons (and perhaps to the amazement of the hypnotists, too), the bleeding has gradually come to a trickling halt.*

Should you be bleeding profusely as a result of the injury, here is what to do mentally:

1. Enter your alpha level.
2. Imagine the bleeding area becoming cold. Feel it getting colder and colder. Imagine it covered with ice. *Know* it is covered with ice.
3. Keep doing this until the bleeding stops. Then end your session.

*As we progress in the book, I will describe many such ways for you to help others, for brain neurons can communicate with other brain neurons *anywhere* where survival is at stake. Still, the first goal is to equip you to care for yourself.

The body obeys the mind. As you hold this cold picture in your mind, the tissues in the bleeding area will actually become cold. They will contract and constrict and the bleeding will stop.

A Summary of Silva Method First-Aid Procedures

Use the following procedure lists as a reference guide for emergency treatment. They are shortened versions of the descriptions given in the several preceding chapters.

Preprogramming Hand Numbness for Pain Control

1. Sit in a straight-backed chair. Go to alpha.
2. Deepen the alpha level with a countdown.
3. Drop your weakest hand into an imaginary bucket of ice-cold water.
4. Permit your hand to get colder and colder for five minutes.
5. Return the hand to your lap and test it by pinching it.
6. Remove the numbness by rubbing your hand three times, wrist out to fingers, mentally saying, "Hand normal."
7. Remind yourself that you can create this numbness whenever necessary in the future by desiring it and that you can pass this numbness to a pained area in your body by contact.
8. End the alpha session.

A Beta or Left-Brain Way to Relieve Pain

1. Point to the pain.
2. Identify its shape and size by describing a container it would best fit.
3. Identify the color of the pain.
4. Identify the taste of the pain.
5. Identify the odor of the pain.
6. Repeat Steps 1 to 5 until the pain has disappeared.

Preprogramming to Activate More of the Mind

1. Go to alpha.
2. Put the thumb and first two fingers of either hand together.
3. Mentally affirm, "Whenever I put these fingers of either hand together, my mind will work at a deeper level of awareness to normalize any illness."
4. End the alpha session.

Preprogramming for Instant Alpha in Case of an Emergency

1. Before falling asleep, go to alpha.
2. Mentally tell yourself to awaken automatically at the best time to program yourself for emergencies.
3. Go to sleep from alpha.
4. When you awaken automatically during the night, go to alpha.
5. Put your three fingers of either hand together.
6. Mentally say, "Whenever I meet with an emergency, all I need to do is defocus my eyes to be at alpha. This will help me to use more of my mind for the best of health."
7. Fall asleep from alpha.

Programming for the Accelerated Healing of Injuries

1. Using the defocusing method if you prefer, go to alpha for fifteen minutes.
2. Picture yourself, as in a full-length mirror, and take two minutes to identify your injuries.
3. Move the picture slightly to the left and imagine healing taking place: cuts mending, bleeding slowing, tissues being restored, broken bones starting to heal. Do this for twelve minutes.
4. Move the picture to the left and imagine yourself healed. Hold the picture for one minute.
5. End your alpha session and repeat twice more during the day and three times a day thereafter (the best times are morning, noon, and night) until healed.

Slowing Profuse Bleeding

1. Using the defocusing method if you prefer, go to alpha.
2. Imagine the bleeding is becoming colder and colder. Feel it cold. Imagine it covered with ice.
3. Keep doing this until the bleeding stops and end the session.

Session 19
The Right Brain and the Positive Approach

1. Close your eyes and roll them slightly upward toward your eyebrows.
2. Steps 2A, 3A, 3B, and 3C are optional. Count slowly and silently from 50 to 1. Wait about one second between numbers.
   A. Starting with your scalp, focus your conscious awareness on the different parts of your body from head to toe, relaxing them as you go.
3. When you reach the count of 1, hold a picture of yourself in your mind as youthful, radiant, healthy, and attractive.
   A. Ask yourself mentally, "Why do I have this physical problem?" Then let your mind wander.
   B. When you find yourself thinking about a certain person, picture that person.
   C. Picture yourself forgiving each other. Imagine a hug or a handshake, smiles, and heads nodding in agreement. Feel good about this.
4. Repeat mentally, "I will always maintain a perfectly healthy body and mind."
5. Say to yourself, "I am going to count from 1 to 5; when I reach the count of 5, I will open my eyes, feeling fine and in perfect health, feeling better than before."
6. Count. When you reach 3, repeat, "When I reach the count of 5, I will open my eyes, feeling fine and in perfect health, feeling better than before."
7. At the count of 5, open your eyes and affirm mentally, "I am wide awake, feeling fine and in perfect health, feeling better than before. And this is so."

The Silva Method is a dual system. You can use it to heal yourself and to heal others. Both types of healing employ positive thinking at the alpha level. Negative thoughts can affect the environment negatively up to a radius of about twenty-five feet. Positive thoughts affect the environment positively but are not limited by distance. Negative thoughts always impede, destroy, or hurt. Positive thoughts always help, create, and heal.

To assist in the immediate area, you need only maintain a positive mental attitude. Your human aura will do the work. This energy radiation from the human body is controlled equally by the left-brain and right-brain hemispheres. However, most of us have learned from the culture to suppress right-brain insights regarding remote or future phenomena as illogical or undependable. Thus, the voices of our right hemispheres hardly ever get through to us except as occasional flashes of insight, perception, intuition, or so-called psychic information and extrasensory perception.

The training and practice you are getting here are helping you to permit your right brain to play a greater role in your life. Your desire, belief, and expectation are allowing you to become a more intuitive person. The longer you allow this process to continue, the more intuitive and perceptive you will become. Allow your right brain to take its rightful place alongside your left brain in making this a better world.

Go to alpha. Visualize your ill health and imagine it being corrected to good health. Your brain frequencies and mental pictures will function as therapeutic tools.

Healing is objective when *physical* means are used to accomplish the work. Healing is subjective when *mental* means are used to accomplish the work. The ideal approach to healing is to use both the subjective and the objective: healing subjectively from the inner layers of matter to the outer and healing objectively from the outer to the inner layers of matter. That is why the Silva Method is best used to complement rather than to substitute for professional health care.

Mining the Unconscious

One of the early pioneers in the study of human consciousness was F. W. H. Myers. He once said that the unconscious mind is "not only a rubbish heap but also a gold mine."

Yes, the subconscious mind is a source of "fight or flight" reactions, of allergies and phobias, of unwanted symptoms and hard-to-break habits. But it is also the source of insight, creative genius, physical perfection, and creative and spiritual impulses that enrich our lives. Together, the alpha level and the Mental Screen enable us to draw from and control our unconscious mind. Remember, the Mental Screen, located about twenty degrees above the horizontal and out and away from the body, is where we do our mental picturing. By picturing yourself on your Mental Screen while you are relaxed, you are projecting the nonphysical counterpart of the physical—its cause or, actually, its energy form.

Afterwards, what you project becomes manifest in the physical form. In this way you can use your imagination to correct unwanted conditions, helping your physician heal you. You heal yourself.

The medical profession is focused on the physical aspects of healing. It has developed a vast array of techniques for combating unwanted physical conditions. It requires years for a doctor to learn how and when to use these techniques and how they work.

The Silva Method focuses on the spiritual aspects of healing. Because it uses the nonphysical, or mental, level, it does not encroach on medical practice. And because doctors use tangible physical methods, they do not ordinarily encroach on the intangible, or spiritual, approaches. The one exception is when doctors use a placebo and harness the power of the patient's mind. By representing the sugar pill as a chemical in the arsenal of healing agents, the doctor is triggering the expectation and belief that healing will take place—and it does.

Silva people welcome such an exception, but we have more precise and effective ways to accomplish this goal than by using a placebo.

Healing Others

Still, it is important to repeat that the Silva Method is not a substitute for medical approaches. Rather, it complements medical approaches. This is an important distinction, particularly as you develop your ability to go to deeper levels of alpha, to use your Mental Screen to make corrections, and to help others heal.

When you help others heal by working in the nonphysical realm, you are not trespassing in the realm of the medical profession. To protect yourself against the accusation of practicing medicine without a license, never work on another person when that person is in your presence. Our millions of graduates are able to quickly enter a deep level of alpha at which healing others becomes possible at a distance. They are able to detect problems intuitively and to make corrections in their imaginations (that is, on the spiritual level), which then manifest on the physical level.

In this way, a graduate helped his neighbor get rid of painful sciatica she had had for years.

A graduate helped an exotic dancer shrink a tumor that was interfering with her performing.

A graduate helped a newborn baby begin to defecate, thus avoiding risky exploratory surgery.

I could fill a book with such examples.

When, as a result of practice, you go to deep alpha, you are a skilled operator. Practice takes you to deep levels of awareness that are controlled not by alpha but by *theta* brain frequencies. Theta frequencies are four to seven cycles per second. The theta dimension controls the autonomic nervous system. It is via this system that cells, tissues, organs, and glands respond to mental messages at alpha.

What this important fact means is that at this deep level of awareness you mentally sit astride the cells and organs of your body and the cells of the body of another person, even at a distance, and can normalize them at will. At deep alpha, with expectation and belief, you can mentally affect the very cells of your body beneficially.

Session 20

Saving Your Life With the Right Brain

1. Close your eyes and roll them slightly upward toward your eyebrows.
2. Steps 2A, 3A, 3B, and 3C are optional. Count slowly and silently from 50 to 1. Wait about one second between numbers.
   A. Starting with your scalp, focus your conscious awareness on the different parts of your body from head to toe, relaxing them as you go.
3. When you reach the count of 1, hold a picture of yourself in your mind as youthful, radiant, healthy, and attractive.
   A. Ask yourself mentally, "Why do I have this physical problem?" Then let your mind wander.
   B. When you find yourself thinking about a certain person, picture that person.
   C. Picture yourself forgiving each other. Imagine a hug or a handshake, smiles, and heads nodding in agreement. Feel good about this.
4. Repeat mentally, "I will always maintain a perfectly healthy body and mind."
5. Say to yourself, "I am going to count from 1 to 5; when I reach the count of 5, I will open my eyes, feeling fine and in perfect health, feeling better than before."
6. Count. When you reach 3, repeat, "When I reach the count of 5, I will open my eyes, feeling fine and in perfect health, feeling better than before."
7. At the count of 5, open your eyes and affirm mentally, "I am wide awake, feeling fine and in perfect health, feeling better than before. And this is so."

Psychosomatic Versus Organic Health Problems

As I asserted earlier, negative thinking weakens the immune system. Fears, anxieties, hostilities, and phobias are just as threatening to health as measles, cholera, tuberculosis, and malaria.

What causes the worry and the other words we give to the negative thinking that weakens the immune system? Life's situations and conflicts, thought about at beta—twenty cycles—is called worrying. Worry and other types of negative thinking weaken the immune system. As the immune system is weakened, vital organs are affected and eventually they go out of balance. Thus, health problems that start out as psychosomatic—without detectable physical basis—frequently become organic, having detectable physical causes.

Take the case of Brad Koblentz. He had a phobia and his phobia could have led to serious physical problems. But he addressed his problems at the alpha level, and this led to a happy ending. Here is his story:

I am a Silva Method Graduate from Judith L. Powell's class. The main reason I took the seminar was because, at that time, I had suffered from agoraphobia for more than twelve years. Agoraphobia is the fear of open spaces. I lived with the fear of having a panic attack, such as rapid breathing, fainting, dying, or falling down. Some people are confined to a safe place, a place where they will feel secure. This may be their home, front yard, town, or just about any place where they are in control, where they can leave quickly if necessary.

I myself could not leave my home town, Brandon, for more than twelve years because I would have an attack. I was never able to drive alone, someone always had to be in the car or truck with me, and I needed to have several objects from my house in the vehicle with me in order to feel comfortable. I had the fear of being afraid!

Many psychologists and behavioral therapists say that the only way to overcome this fear is to face it. However, the most difficult part of overcoming agoraphobia is taking that first step.

Through the use of the Silva Method techniques, I have been able to leave the fears behind me.

When I begin a trip of any distance, I pretend to see the entire trip scene in my mirror—I see myself safe and feeling relaxed. I program a wonderful, restful trip.

Also, if any negative thoughts occur or if my fears of panic attacks start creeping in while I'm at level, I say, "Cancel, cancel!" and go to an imagined place of relaxation.

Then, while on the trip, if I start to have any negative thoughts, or begin any "What if" statements, I say out loud, "Cancel, cancel," and use the Three-Fingers Technique to go to my place of relaxation. This technique has worked and will work every time to help me become more calm and restful.

Brad Koblentz could have developed any number of psychosomatic health problems, and these in turn could have produced serious physical symptoms. For instance, his chronic worry could have caused an alteration of his gastric juices, which could have brought about peptic ulcers. But when he began to analyze his problem in the midspan of brain-wave frequencies—namely, alpha—both brain hemispheres became involved in creating a solution.

Why are we not taught to do this in school? It is so important to the health of humanity. It is so simple, so effective, and so quick.

Psychosomatic health problems are not imaginary to the patient. They are real. They may start in the imagination, but because the imagination is creative, they become real health problems. Frequently the physician cannot detect these health problems, because he or she is looking objectively, from outer toward inner. Because these health problems have started subjectively, they may still be at the inner layers of matter and may not have yet reached the outer layers. The person with psychosomatic health problems in the initial states is, therefore, his or her own best therapist.

The Life-Saving Right Hemisphere

Research and clinical evidence point increasingly to the fact that all disease is psychosomatic, and that by changing your mind you can change your health – for better or worse. But is a broken leg really psychosomatic? Is a fractured skull psychosomatic? The answer that is emerging from a number of research frontiers is yes.

One day it may be much clearer to us, but meanwhile a number of psychological, physiological, and philosophical signs *seem* at least to point to one conclusion: there is no such thing as an accident. A drunken driver slams head-on into a family on their way to church. Five people are killed. The drunken driver is barely shaken up. Is this not purely an accident, and a totally tragic one at that?

Behind the Higher Intelligence that runs the universe are purposes and ends that we cannot possibly know. Still, we can know more than we do today. We have a hot line to Higher Intelligence. It is our right-brain hemisphere. When we activate the right hemisphere of our brain, we are activating our intuitive faculty, what we might refer to as our gut feelings.

Why did a lady decide to take a later plane, only to read later that the first one had crashed?

Why did a man decide to take a longer route this time, only to find out later that the bridge on the short route was washed out?

Gut feeling. Intuition. Right-brain input. Right-brain activity is heightened at the alpha level.

You are already activating intuitive measures for your survival in your morning countdown exercises. When you have completed those exercises, a simple countdown from 5 to 1 with eyes closed and turned slightly upward will be just as effective as counting from 100 to 1 or 50 to 1 in bringing you to alpha level. If you have preprogrammed yourself as described earlier, you will be able to put your thumb and two fingers together to trigger more dependable intuitive decisions, and you will be able to defocus your eyes to do likewise.

So alpha can be a life saver, by keeping you out of trouble.

Session 21
Eliminating Pernicious Thoughts

1. Close your eyes and roll them slightly upward toward your eyebrows.
2. You are now ready to reduce your count from 50 to 1 to 25 to 1. Count slowly and silently from 25 to 1. Wait about one second between numbers. Steps 2A, 3A, 3B, and 3C are optional.
   A. Starting with your scalp, focus your conscious awareness on the different parts of your body from head to toe, relaxing them as you go.
3. When you reach the count of 1, hold a picture of yourself in your mind as youthful, radiant, healthy, and attractive.
   A. Ask yourself mentally, "Why do I have this physical problem?" Then let your mind wander.
   B. When you find yourself thinking about a certain person, picture that person.
   C. Picture yourself forgiving each other. Imagine a hug or a handshake, smiles, and heads nodding in agreement. Feel good about this.
4. Repeat mentally, "I will always maintain a perfectly healthy body and mind."
5. Say to yourself, "I am going to count from 1 to 5; when I reach the count of 5, I will open my eyes, feeling fine and in perfect health, feeling better than before."
6. Count. When you reach 3, repeat, "When I reach the count of 5, I will open my eyes, feeling fine and in perfect health, feeling better than before."
7. At the count of 5, open your eyes and affirm mentally, "I am wide awake, feeling fine and in perfect health, feeling better than before. And this is so."

The Negative Power of Destructive Thoughts

Henry Thoreau wrote, "Most men lead lives of quiet desperation." He must have meant women, too. If not, he would certainly include women today. Contemporary men and women face problems and situations that test their very will to live. Suicide hot lines buzz throughout our country, and for every such telephone call that is made, there are a thousand silent calls of quiet desperation.

Add to suicidal thoughts those thoughts that are so negative and destructive that they can lead to stroke, heart attack, self-inflicted injury, attacks, and even murder, and you get a volume of off-center thinking that adds up to most of the troubles of the world.

The rectification starts at home. It starts in your mind.

Who can claim to be entirely free of negative thoughts? Even the smallest thought of destruction can claim its piece of reality. Such a thought must be stopped in its tracks. How? You already know how.

If you ever experience a destructive thought toward yourself or others, at that moment, or as soon after that moment as is possible, go to your alpha level and do this immediately:

1. At alpha, identify the destructive thought(s) you have just experienced.
2. Mentally tell yourself, "I don't need to have these thoughts; I don't want to have these thoughts; I will no longer have these thoughts."
3. End your session.

In a variation of this method, you can program yourself so that whenever a hideous thought is about to enter your head, it will be replaced by another, more desirable thought. To effect this replacement, you must select the more desirable thought to be used as the substitute. This desirable thought must be of a more spiritual, and therefore more creative, genre. Ideal thoughts would be of Jesus, Buddha, or God—whatever idea is the highest in your philosophy or religion. The procedure would then be as follows:

1. At alpha, identify the destructive thought(s).
2. Mentally tell yourself, "I don't need to have these thoughts; I don't want to have these thoughts, and from now on, should these thoughts begin to enter my mind, I will instead think of [insert spiritual choice]."
3. End your session.

To reinforce either variation, you can use the Three-Fingers Technique described earlier. Program yourself with the idea that whenever destructive thoughts appear, you will put your thumb and the first two fingers of either hand together and the unwanted thoughts will disappear. In the future, when you find yourself becoming destructive in your thinking, put your thumb and first two fingers of either hand together and your thoughts will automatically change for the better.

Here is the procedure for programming in this way:

1. Go to your alpha level and deepen it with a 10 to 1 extra countdown.
2. Identify the destructive thoughts you want to stop thinking.
3. Put the thumb together with the first two fingers of either hand.
4. Repeat mentally, "Whenever I put these three fingers of either hand together, my mind functions at a deeper, more positive level."
5. End your alpha session.
6. Whenever negative thoughts begin, immediately put your thumb and first two fingers of either hand together.

You can program this technique at the most effective time for you by going to your alpha level just before falling asleep and programming that you will awaken automatically at that time. When you awaken for the first time that night, follow Steps 1 through 4.

You can combine the variation with the reinforcement by adding these words at the end of Step 4: "and my thoughts turn to [insert spiritual choice]."

Attack Problems Early

Negative thoughts that are not intense enough to merit the term *destructive* can still cloud an event or a relationship, and if they are held chronically they can eventually evolve into more pernicious states of mind. To counteract this tendency, you can use the simple basic technique of going to your alpha level, identifying the problem, asserting when you open your eyes at the count of 5 that the problem will be gone, and counting yourself out. The earlier you do this the better. Whether a headache, an epileptic attack, an asthma attack, or mild depression will be the end result, it is best to program the possibility away as soon as you feel the first unpleasant sensations or think the first unpleasant thoughts.

Using the Thymus Technique

However, if it is not possible to go to your alpha level, or if you have not preprogrammed the Three-Fingers Technique, there is a quick, effective procedure. Tap your thymus gland and put a smile on your face.

If you *have* already programmed the Three-Fingers Technique, simply tap your thymus gland with the programmed three fingers. The thymus gland is about one and one-half inches below the point where the soft neck tissue meets the sternum, or breastbone. Silva graduates have been learning this method for quite some time, even before scientists determined the exact function of the thymus gland. Now the thymus gland is understood to be a sort of master regulator of other glands, systems, and organs.

Recently, researchers found that simply smiling triggers the brain to release chemicals such as endorphins—chemicals that themselves cause you to smile. In other words, the tail can wag the dog. When you feel good, you smile. But when you smile, you feel good.

Here, then, is an instant way to set yourself up at the beta level, since the method is objective. It is a direct physical cause-effect action. You can reinforce its effectiveness by preprogramming the Three-Fingers Technique for deeper mental awareness. With or without that technique, here is the procedure:

1. Immediately upon feeling any negative or physical mental state, smile.
2. Put the thumb and first two fingers of either hand together.
3. Vigorously tap your thymus gland with one set of fingers for about half a minute.

Here are some examples of the types of problems this procedure can help:

- Dizziness
- Fatigue
- Boredom
- Exasperation
- Depression
- The morning "blahs"
- Apathy
- Impatience
- Disorientation
- Pessimism

Session 22
A Fantastic Voyage

1. Close your eyes and roll them slightly upward toward your eyebrows.
2. Steps 2A, 3A, 3B, and 3C are optional. Count from 25 to 1. Count slowly and silently. Wait about one second between numbers.
   A. Starting with your scalp, focus your conscious awareness on the different parts of your body from head to toe, relaxing them as you go.
3. When you reach the count of 1, hold a picture of yourself in your mind as youthful, radiant, healthy, and attractive.
   A. Ask yourself mentally, "Why do I have this physical problem?" Then let your mind wander.
   B. When you find yourself thinking about a certain person, picture that person.
   C. Picture yourself forgiving each other. Imagine a hug or a handshake, smiles, and heads nodding in agreement. Feel good about this.
4. Repeat mentally, "I will always maintain a perfectly healthy body and mind."
5. Say to yourself, "I am going to count from 1 to 5; when I reach the count of 5, I will open my eyes, feeling fine and in perfect health, feeling better than before."
6. Count. When you reach 3, repeat, "When I reach the count of 5, I will open my eyes, feeling fine and in perfect health, feeling better than before."
7. At the count of 5, open your eyes and affirm mentally, "I am wide awake, feeling fine and in perfect health, feeling better than before. And this is so."

Each morning when you practice your countdown exercises, you get closer and closer to deep alpha. You are aiming for ten cycles per second (CPS)—that is, the brain frequency called the centered frequency level, or, in the Silva Method, the ten CPS. The centered frequency level of ten CPS is where more of your mind is activated and where, therefore, effective programming can take place.

However, your mind is constantly being programmed by the external environment while you are at the beta level (a brain frequency of fourteen to twenty-one pulsations per second). It takes repetition for this to happen, but happen it does.

You are programmed by events that repeat themselves, by statements that you hear repeatedly, by advertisements and commercials that appear regularly in the media. You can program yourself by doing something over and over, such as hitting the typewriter keys. At first you might type only ten to twenty words a minute, but with simple practice you go faster and faster. Eventually, you have programmed yourself to be a typist. Similarly, you can program yourself to ride a bicycle, to bowl, to drive a car. Programming at the beta level is called objective learning. Programming at the alpha level is called subjective learning.

Even though you may not have completed your morning practice sessions, you can begin to program yourself now for better health. This programming will take place at some frequency beween high beta and low alpha, depending on your stage of practice and your relaxation skills. The programming will require repetition to be successful. The higher your brain frequency, the more repetition it will take.

One way to proceed is to sit in a comfortable chair, close your eyes, turn them slightly upward, and repeat the morning phrase, "I will always maintain a perfectly healthy body and mind," holding in your mind a picture of yourself as radiantly healthy, vigorous, and attractive. Another way is to go on a "fantastic voyage."

Some years ago a motion picture by that name caused quite a stir. It involved a team of medical scientists who were miniaturized to travel inside a living human being. You can imagine yourself taking a trip inside your own body, gaining health benefits from the "voyage."

Where consciousness goes, energy goes. If you hear about a disease and you daydream about the possibility of your contracting it, you are beginning to attract it, even to create it. Repeat this frequently enough and you will be called a hypochondriac. The hypochondriac who constantly imagines being sick can develop the very symptoms feared.

The opposite is also true.

Imagine yourself healthy; do this frequently at beta and you will create what you imagine. It takes a while at beta, longer than at alpha, but mental pictures are creative at any level.

Imagine you are inside your own body. Admire your heart, that twenty-four-hour pumping station; or your brain, that amazing computer; or your stomach, that ingenious chemical factory, which digests any combination of foods you put into it. Through your admiration of these organs, you will be sending positive energy to them. They "know" you are thinking kindly of them. They "appreciate" it.

And they respond.

You do not have to know the ins and outs of human anatomy to benefit from this mental exercise. Your concept of a heart or a liver or a kidney will identify that organ satisfactorily, and you will not get a "wrong number."

This trip will be more enjoyable and effective if you do not have to stop and think about what to do next. A way to solve this problem is to have somebody read the instructions to you (the instructions are in the following section). Or you could make a cassette tape, relax, and listen to it.

Here is the procedure:

1. Sit in a comfortable chair, close your eyes, turn them slightly upward, and count backward as you did this morning.

2. When you reach the count of 1, turn on the cassette or tell your reader to begin.
3. After completing the imaginary internal voyage, count yourself out as you do in the morning.

Instructions for a Fantastic Voyage

Relax. Take a deep breath. As you exhale, relax your body and go deeper.

Turn your awareness to your scalp. Picture the hair penetrating the scalp. Send your awareness down one of the hairs to below the scalp. There you find a forest of hair roots. Thank your hair for being your crowning glory. Thank your scalp for its protection. Have your scalp send a word of thanks to all the skin cells for doing such a great service to your body. Go a little deeper with your awareness and be aware of your skull. Thank your skull for its heroic work. Have your skull send thanks to all the bone cells for providing the skeletal structure for your body.

Go still a little deeper with your awareness into the brain level. Send sincere thank yous and words of appreciation to your brain, a marvelous organ of intelligence, a computer that runs your body and provides you with the means to manifest your intellect. Going deeper still into the body, thank your eyes for the sense of sight, your nose for its respiratory function and sense of smell, your mouth and tongue for the sense of taste and digestive function.

As you imagine yourself sliding down your throat into your stomach, thank your stomach for its digestive capability, a tip of the hat to this great chemical laboratory able to digest all combinations of foods you put into it.

Surrounding the stomach are the liver, pancreas, spleen, and gallbladder. Thank these organs for the contributions they make to digestion and other bodily functions. At the outlet of the stomach, you enter the small intestine. It is a twisting, turning trip from there to the large intestine. Thank your small intestine for its job in continuing the digestive process and in the absorp-

tion of nutrients. When you enter the large intestine, or colon, where the appendix is located, thank your large intestine for its garbage disposal work, a thankless job but a vital one.

While in this area of the body, thank your kidneys for cleaning your blood of poisons and their garbage disposal work; thank your reproductive organs; thank your abdominal muscles and have them send the word of thanks and appreciation to all the rest of the muscles and tissues.

Now, enter a vein or artery and ride along in the bloodstream. Thank the veins and arteries for remaining clean so as to provide good circulation of the blood to all parts of your body. Thank the bloodstream, the red blood corpuscles, and especially the white blood corpuscles, which act as the police of the blood system. Thank them for keeping you immune from disease.

Emerge temporarily from the blood when it reaches your lungs. Thank your lungs for supplying oxygen to your blood to feed the body and for eliminating poisons. Back in your bloodstream, then alight more once when you reach the heart. Give a sincere thank you to the heart for its twenty-four-hour work as a pumping station for your blood.

Back in your bloodstream, disembark under your scalp, shimmy up a hair, and arrive once more outside your body. Count yourself out in your usual manner, feeling wide awake as you open your eyes, better than before.

Session 23
Your Self-Concept

1. Close your eyes and roll them slightly upward toward your eyebrows.
2. Steps 2A, 3A, 3B, and 3C are optional. Count from 25 to 1. Count slowly and silently. Wait about one second between numbers.
   A. Starting with your scalp, focus your conscious awareness on the different parts of your body from head to toe, relaxing them as you go.
3. When you reach the count of 1, hold a picture of yourself in your mind as youthful, radiant, healthy, and attractive.
   A. Ask yourself mentally, "Why do I have this physical problem?" Then let your mind wander.
   B. When you find yourself thinking about a certain person, picture that person.
   C. Picture yourself forgiving each other. Imagine a hug or a handshake, smiles, and heads nodding in agreement. Feel good about this.
4. Repeat mentally, "I will always maintain a perfectly healthy body and mind."
5. Say to yourself, "I am going to count from 1 to 5; when I reach the count of 5, I will open my eyes, feeling fine and in perfect health, feeling better than before."
6. Count. When you reach 3, repeat, "When I reach the count of 5, I will open my eyes, feeling fine and in perfect health, feeling better than before."
7. At the count of 5, open your eyes and affirm mentally, "I am wide awake, feeling fine and in perfect health, feeling better than before. And this is so."

Your Self-Concept, Your Body, and Your Behavior

When D.K. began taking the Silva training, she was suffering from severe hypoglycemic anxiety symptoms—fainting spells, dizziness, and adrenaline surges. In two weeks these symptoms started to diminish. In two months they were gone.

But what was even more important to D.K. was that she found herself. "For the past ten years, I have been searching for the spiritual key that would unlock the treasures in my soul. . . . The Silva Method has given me the direction and the confidence."

Psychological testing of Silva graduates has shown that they are more accepting of their physical self-image—their appearance and stature. They perceive themselves as much healthier than before. They also perceive themselves as better able to get along with and care for members of their own families. And they perceive themselves as better able to get along with other people.

What happens in people's lives when they see themselves as healthier and better able to work with others? They *are* healthier and they become more productive at work and at home.

What happens when they

- value themselves more highly?
- are less critical and negative?
- are more accepting of themselves?
- are more creative?
- have a better memory?

These attributes are all increased by the Silva training, as standardized before-and-after testing shows. Students show an enhanced self-concept, and an enhanced self-concept produces an enhanced human being.

The Silva Method for Personality Improvement

As scientific as the Silva Method is, there is no mistaking its spiritual implications. Perhaps it is for this reason that the parochial schools on Guam have recently begun to train their faculty and student bodies in the Silva Method. Influencing their decision were the results of similar projects in parochial schools on the United States mainland.

Projects at these schools were supervised by Dr. George T. DeSau and utilized before-and-after testing with standardized personality tests: the Cattell 16 Personality Factors test, used in adult populations, and the HSPQ, in high school populations, both published by the Institute for Personality and Ability Testing.

Here are the key findings:

- In nearly all groups tested, subjects showed a strong movement away from being easily upset and toward "high ego strength, mature, faces reality, calm."
- The stability of this heightened ego strength was demonstrated by follow-up testing four and five months after the training. Indeed, further increases showed at this time.

Other research projects have been carried out with the Silva Method training in Albuquerque, New Mexico, and Ottawa County, Michigan. Here are some key findings:

- There was a significant shift in adults away from "apprehensive, self-reproaching, worrying, troubled" and toward "self-assured, placid, serene."
- The development of an inner-conscious direction released inhibiting factors in social interaction. A test group of adults, using the 16 PF test, shifted away from "shy, timid, threat-sensitive" toward "spontaneous, socially bold."
- A shift characteristic of a majority of the testing projects has been away from "tense, frustrated, driven, overwrought" toward "relaxed, tranquil, unfrustrated, composed."
- There was movement away from "reserved, detached, critical, aloof" toward "warm, outgoing, participating."

- Tests showed participants were less suspicious, mistrustful, and competitive, and instead showed a greater willingness to work with others.
- There was a newfound freedom from previous anxieties and inner turmoil, demonstrated by a movement in the test results away from gloominess and pessimism toward greater cheerfulness, enthusiasm, and *joie de vivre.*

To summarize, the list on the left below shows the traits diminished by the Silva Method and the list on the right shows the traits enhanced:

Traits Diminished	*Traits Enhanced*
Easily upset	High ego strength
Apprehensive	Mature
Self-reproaching	Faces reality
Worrying	Calm
Shy	Self-assured
Timid	Placid
Threat-sensitive	Serene
Tense	Spontaneous
Frustrated	Socially bold
Driven	Relaxed
Overwrought	Tranquil
Reserved	Unfrustrated
Detached	Composed
Critical	Warm
Aloof	Outgoing
Suspicious	Participating
Competitive	Cooperative
Gloomy	Cheerful
Pessimistic	Enthusiastic

Read the left-hand column. Are these traits you would admire in yourself?

Now read the right-hand column. Do these describe more accurately the way you want to be?

Graduates of the Silva Method who were tested showed a movement from the left column to the right column.

In practicing your countdown exercises for forty mornings, you will be gradually making this shift. The more you use your alpha level, the more you will demonstrate the personality traits in the right-hand column in your everyday life.

Session 24
Healing Without Intention

1. Close your eyes and roll them slightly upward toward your eyebrows.
2. Steps 2A, 3A, 3B, and 3C are optional. Count from 25 to 1. Count slowly and silently. Wait about one second between numbers.
   A. Starting with your scalp, focus your conscious awareness on the different parts of your body from head to toe, relaxing them as you go.
3. When you reach the count of 1, hold a picture of yourself in your mind as youthful, radiant, healthy, and attractive.
   A. Ask yourself mentally, "Why do I have this physical problem?" Then let your mind wander.
   B. When you find yourself thinking about a certain person, picture that person.
   C. Picture yourself forgiving each other. Imagine a hug or a handshake, smiles, and heads nodding in agreement. Feel good about this.
4. Repeat mentally, "I will always maintain a perfectly healthy body and mind."
5. Say to yourself, "I am going to count from 1 to 5; when I reach the count of 5, I will open my eyes, feeling fine and in perfect health, feeling better than before."
6. Count. When you reach 3, repeat, "When I reach the count of 5, I will open my eyes, feeling fine and in perfect health, feeling better than before."
7. At the count of 5, open your eyes and affirm mentally, "I am wide awake, feeling fine and in perfect health, feeling better than before. And this is so."

There is the possibility that merely learning to go to alpha will heal you.

G.S., a lady about sixty, told one of our lecturers, "If I walk out of the room, it's not because I'm bored; I have had colitis for years and I get sudden calls to go to the bathroom."

"I understand," replied the lecturer. "But don't be surprised if that does not happen at all."

It did not happen at all. Just by going to alpha and programming positive thoughts during training, the woman cured herself of colitis.

Another woman, Louise Owen, was told in September 1980 that she was dying. For more than a year she had been ill with hepatitis. Now, her doctor was ready to give up. The hepatitis had taken over the whole body and could not be arrested.

She was attracted to a book on the Silva Method. After reading it, she looked up Silva in the telephone directory and signed up for a course to be given over two weekends.

Writes Louise Owen:

During the week between the two halves of the series, I had an appointment with my doctor. He took another blood test and could not believe what he found: clear blood!

So he took a second test, and this confirmed the first.

He couldn't understand how anyone could be healed of a terminal case of hepatitis in a week! But he had to admit I was well.

Now, more than a year later, I am still healthy.

The first half of the Silva training includes a dozen alpha-level sessions averaging fifteen minutes each. Besides alpha-deepening and problem-solving techniques, these "conditioning cycles" also specifically address insomnia, headaches, and fatigue.

How, then, did these conditioning cycles help Louise Owen with hepatitis?

The cycles contain positive affirmations that will help you learn not to get certain illnesses, but hepatitis is not one of those mentioned. However, included in the cycles is this general positive affirmation: "I will always maintain a perfectly healthy body and mind."

I point this out to emphasize the importance of the alpha level and a climate of positive thought. In thousands of instances, minor ailments and complaints vanish in the course of the training without the subject ever using any methodology.

A woman with chronic neuralgia in her face for a period of years reports to the class midway through the training that she is free of that pain.

An insurance salesman who keeps asking throughout the class sessions how he can rid his hand of arthritis, demonstrating each time how his fingers will not close, suddenly exclaims, "My arthritis is gone," and shows the class that it is so.

This is not to say you should forget the methodology and simply remain at alpha. But do not throw up your hands at applying the methodology for your special health problem just because the illness seems complicated or the psychology of the health problem is not completely understood.

Dive in. Do it. Do whatever comes to you to do. Spend fifteen minutes at alpha. Visualize yourself as you are now. Move the picture to the left and fix yourself up. Move the picture to the left again and imagine yourself perfect.

Session 25
Improving Visualization

1. Close your eyes and roll them slightly upward toward your eyebrows.
2. Steps 2A, 3A, 3B, and 3C are optional. Count from 25 to 1. Count slowly and silently. Wait about one second between numbers.
   A. Starting with your scalp, focus your conscious awareness on the different parts of your body from head to toe, relaxing them as you go.
3. When you reach the count of 1, hold a picture of yourself in your mind as youthful, radiant, healthy, and attractive.
   A. Ask yourself mentally, "Why do I have this physical problem?" Then let your mind wander.
   B. When you find yourself thinking about a certain person, picture that person.
   C. Picture yourself forgiving each other. Imagine a hug or a handshake, smiles, and heads nodding in agreement. Feel good about this.
4. Repeat mentally, "I will always maintain a perfectly healthy body and mind."
5. Say to yourself, "I am going to count from 1 to 5; when I reach the count of 5, I will open my eyes, feeling fine and in perfect health, feeling better than before."
6. Count. When you reach 3, repeat, "When I reach the count of 5, I will open my eyes, feeling fine and in perfect health, feeling better than before."
7. At the count of 5, open your eyes and affirm mentally, "I am wide awake, feeling fine and in perfect health, feeling better than before. And this is so."

Improving Visualization for Better Results

At a recent institute on visualization and healing held at an annual meeting of the Association for Humanistic Psychology, Robin Casarjian, who is a psychotherapist specializing in stress management at the Harvard Medical Plan at Massachusetts General Hospital, was asked if visualization involved self-hypnosis. She replied that when we visualize, we are *de*hypnotizing ourselves.

How true! When we relax, we activate the right brain. When we visualize, we utilize the right and left brain. We are more alert, more intelligent, more in control. This is quite the opposite of being hypnotized. The better we relax and the better we visualize, the better we heal.

Remember, it is not necessary to visualize in wide-screen Technicolor or in minutest detail. However deeply you do relax, however well you visualize, be comfortable with that and proceed with your healing work. In time you will relax more deeply. In time you will visualize in more detail. But meanwhile, why not take advantage of the improved health possible by applying these skills at whatever level they have developed so far?

It will only get better and better.

Certain exercises will help you improve your visualization skills. Because visualizing yourself is essential to healing yourself, you should practice what is called the mirror exercise. Look at yourself in a mirror, close your eyes, and recall your face. Then open your eyes to see how well you did. If the nose, lips, eyebrows were not perfect, examine them closely in the mirror. Then close your eyes again and visualize your face. Open your eyes. Check your face. This time you should have done better.

In another, more general exercise, visualize something mentioned in a conversation or that you have read in a book. For example, your friend has just mentioned his car. Imagine his car. Think about what it looks like. Doing so will not interrupt the conversation. An author describes a house. Imagine what this house looks like. It will not interfere with your reading. The more you visualize and imagine, the more adept you will become in being creative. In this case, you yourself are the creator. Your health is being created.

How Visualization Triggers Healing Energy

When you think of walking to a door, that thought is not cast into words. There is an instant in which you hold that event in your mind. You imagine yourself walking to the door.

The instantaneous picture serves as a demand on the computer. The computer, your brain, is asked to cause the body to produce the energy necessary to move your specific body weight the specific distance and to produce the necessary leg movement to accomplish the event. So your brain institutes the required change in body chemistry and the required muscle movement. When you stop to think about this simple act, it is really a marvelous ability.

Healing is no more marvelous. It, too, makes a simple demand on the computer brain that is initiated by a mental picture. When the picture of healing is held in the mind, the necessary body changes are activated by the computer brain and the event is accomplished.

You know how to walk to a door. Merely by changing the mental picture, you can channel the energy required to do so to reach a healthy goal instead of reaching a door. But the analogy holds. When you want to go to the door, you make the decision to do it now. You take it for granted that walking will get you there. You walk; you get there. You want to get well. You make the decision to get well again. You take it for granted that alpha imagination will help you get well. You go to alpha and imagine. You get well.

What are the exact cause-effect links in the chain between imagining the immune system defeating the bacterial invaders and having that event actually take place? Let us leave that question to the psychoneuroimmunologists.

Go to your alpha level. Visualize yourself with your problem. Visualizing means remembering with your mind what you have already seen with your eyes or imagined with your mind (as opposed to imagining, which is picturing with your mind what you have not yet seen with your eyes or imagined before). You have seen your body with its problem, so you have no difficulty visualizing—that is, remembering what something you have seen looks like.

The next step is making mental corrections in the problem area. If this involves something you have never seen before, such as a skin graft in the case of a burn, a kidney stone being pulverized, or an army of white blood cells going into battle, then simply imagine what it looks like. Use the word *imagine* instead of *visualize*, because your eye has never seen the phenomenon in question, nor have you ever imagined it before. You have to pretend that you know what it looks like. You have to make up the picture.

What if the picture is not anatomically correct? It does not matter. Your brain gets the message, because the concept is there and it is the *concept* of the healing that does the programming. Mental pictures are the language of concepts.

It is impossible to cover in this book mental pictures applying to every health problem. But when you understand the simple principle behind using mental pictures for physical healing, you can carry the ball yourself in any situation.

Visualization Versus Imagination in Healing

Some people are more comfortable visualizing than imagining. To them, imagining feels like guessing, and they don't like to make the wrong guess.

In healing, it does not matter if you make the wrong guess; your brain knows what you mean. But what does matter is that you are comfortable with what you are doing.

Not being comfortable with imagining is a way of saying that you have doubts, and doubt subverts. So you must be comfortable with what you are doing.

Now I am going to let you in on something about your imagination that may come as a shock.

An Unusual Ability of the Imagination

It has been found that when the imagination creates a picture it has never before seen, that picture bears a remarkable resemblance to reality. Let me put this another way. We are able to detect information outside of the range of our optical vision with the use of our imagination.

If this seems "far out," let me refer you to the work called "remote viewing" that went on at SRI International in Menlo Park, California, for more than ten years. This multimillion-dollar program, which had the support of the United States government, explored techniques that would make this perceptual ability more accurate and reliable. Participants in this research, as well as in similar research conducted in more than a score of other organizational projects, learned to describe objects, buildings, geographical areas, and activities up to thousands of miles away. The accuracy of their description was frequently as high as 80 percent, even among previously inexperienced people.

The chief conclusion that emerged from this research is that accuracy improved with practice. Practice provides feedback. No skill has ever been learned by humans without feedback. We learn to walk by trial and error. The error—a fall—provides information to the brain's cortex, and the brain learns to avoid the error in the future. In learning to talk, our ears give us feedback. Similarly, we can only learn to play a musical instrument by practicing, during which we receive auditory feedback.

The mind as healer thrives on feedback. You relax and picture positively. You fail to activate the healing process. Again you relax and picture positively. This time you heal. You have learned through feedback. Perhaps you relaxed in a different way the second time, or perhaps you imagined more clearly, or perhaps you spent more time at it. Whatever you did differently during this experience became part of your improved skill, thanks to the feedback the practice provided.

The amazing truth is that you and I are able to project our intelligence any distance at will and know things we have no way of knowing through the senses. The simple key: relax and use the imagination.

The explanation: activating the right hemisphere of the brain appears to help us transcend the objective limitations of time and space.

We do not use this special attribute of the imagination in healing ourselves, but we find it useful in healing other people.

Visualizing Internal "Movies"

S.M. was fourteen years old. She had suffered from asthma for more than ten years. Because her mother was a registered nurse and her father an X-ray technician, they were allowed to keep Adrenalin in their home to control her attacks. Still, S.M. had to go to the hospital frequently for emergency treatment. Her father had read about the Silva Method and decided he would try to help his daughter help herself. The mother was skeptical, but agreed not to interfere.

When the next attack occurred, here is the procedure that the father led his daughter through:

Imagine you are inside your body. Picture your lungs. They are gray pink instead of bright pink. Not enough air is coming in. Look, there is a creature in your lungs. He has his hand on a lever. On one side of the handle it says Unhealthy, *on the other side,* Healthy. *It is on the unhealthy side now. This creature is a playful imp. Let's play with him. Take a big breath and see what happens. [The deep breath makes S.M. cough.] Wow. That air tickled him. Look.*

He has moved the handle a little bit toward healthy. See, your lungs look pinker. Let's see what happens if you take three deep breaths. [Again S.M. coughs on each breath.] See. He has moved the lever toward healthy again. Look at your lungs; they are even pinker.

Her father left the room at this point, instructing S.M. to continue on her own. He returned in about fifteen minutes and asked where the handle was. S.M. replied that it was three-quarters of the way to healthy. After a total of forty-five minutes of breathing and imagining in this manner, S.M. reported the handle at healthy. At this point S.M. went to bed and quickly fell asleep and a trip to the hospital had been avoided.

From then on S.M. used visualization and imagination herself. Whenever she felt an attack coming on, she would isolate herself, perhaps by going to her room, and would use the visualizing and imagining technique. She reported that she would usually recover in five to ten minutes.

The idea here is to devise mental movies that portray a problem, the correction, and the happy ending. One woman used the Radio City Rockettes as a mental scene. They were kicking. With each kick, they ousted more germs. A man pictured his white blood cells as navy frogmen capturing the invading bacteria. You are the screenwriter, producer, and director. What you see in the mental movie you create. Here are the steps:

1. Go to your alpha level.
2. Imagine you are inside your body at the trouble spot.
3. Action! The trouble is being corrected.
4. There is no more trouble.
5. End your session.

Session 26
Stopping Unwanted Habits

1. Close your eyes and roll them slightly upward toward your eyebrows.
2. Steps 2A, 3A, 3B, and 3C are optional. Count from 25 to 1. Count slowly and silently. Wait about one second between numbers.
   A. Starting with your scalp, focus your conscious awareness on the different parts of your body from head to toe, relaxing them as you go.
3. When you reach the count of 1, hold a picture of yourself in your mind as youthful, radiant, healthy, and attractive.
   A. Ask yourself mentally, "Why do I have this physical problem?" Then let your mind wander.
   B. When you find yourself thinking about a certain person, picture that person.
   C. Picture yourself forgiving each other. Imagine a hug or a handshake, smiles, and heads nodding in agreement. Feel good about this.
4. Repeat mentally, "I will always maintain a perfectly healthy body and mind."
5. Say to yourself, "I am going to count from 1 to 5; when I reach the count of 5, I will open my eyes, feeling fine and in perfect health, feeling better than before."
6. Count. When you reach 3, repeat, "When I reach the count of 5, I will open my eyes, feeling fine and in perfect health, feeling better than before."
7. At the count of 5, open your eyes and affirm mentally, "I am wide awake, feeling fine and in perfect health, feeling better than before. And this is so."

Hope for Alcoholics

A study was recently conducted with a group of fifteen recovering alcoholics at the request of the director of an alcohol treatment halfway house. Thirteen men and two women who completed a standard personality questionnaire (16 PF Cattell) took the Silva Method training and then completed the questionnaire again.

The testing was administered by a psychologist who himself took the training along with the alcoholics. The questionnaire measures sixteen personality traits.

The results showed that one change in the personalities of the participants had to do with their ego strength. This factor is important in that it relates to how successfully or unsuccessfully we cope with situations facing us in life. Often, a low ego strength indicates existing pathology.

The posttesting of the participants showed a shift toward strong ego strength—which meant that the alcoholics perceived themselves to be more inner-directed than outer-directed, a sign of good mental health and emotional stability. Inner-directed people, because of their capacity to choose based on their own expectations of themselves, seem better able to exert self-control over their behavior and life paths. Also shown in the posttest was a shift from controlling, self-serving behavior to a more forthright, unpretentious, nonmanipulative stance. And those studied showed increased qualities of almost naive emotional genuineness, complete directness, and spontaneous outspokenness.

The participants further showed a shift toward more self-confidence and self-guidance. Reliance on inner assurance is seen as replacing dependence on external reinforcement. The recovering group reported more self-assurance in their ability to deal with any situation that might arise. Accompanying this change was a shift in self-perception away from being "shy, inhibited and threat-sensitive" and toward being more "adventuresome and socially bold."

The area of threat sensitivity may be of considerable importance in understanding the behavior of the alcoholic. It is very possible that alcoholics use alcohol as a means of attempting to balance out their mental/physical systems. An improved self-concept and ability to handle anxiety would seem to be a meaningful alternative to alcohol.

In other personality areas, the study showed a significant shift toward "a relaxed, tranquil, unfrustrated and composed state," one that contrasted with a "tense, frustrated" condition. The diminished inner struggles reflected by the group's response to questionnaire items perhaps indicated the individuals' perception of themselves as having achieved more control of inner processes.

Six months after the completion of the Silva Method training, a follow-up was conducted with the fifteen recovering alcoholics tested. Of the fifteen, twelve had consumed no alcohol whatsoever during the interim. One individual had taken a glass of wine and stopped; one had twice started drinking but managed to stop without becoming intoxicated to the point of requiring hospitalization; and one required hospitalization for the excessive consumption of alcohol.

The correction for alcoholism, then, is not merely to picture the hand empty of a shot glass. The correction includes strengthening weak personality traits that precipitate reliance on that shot glass. This means giving yourself positive programming to strengthen such factors as self-concept, self-assurance, and self-reliance.

You can mentally affirm these positive commands while you imagine a second picture. Visualize yourself responding to these positive commands. You stand straighter. You radiate a new determination. You turn up your nose at the taste of liquor. Your eyes shine with a new light.

Now you are ready for that third picture: you live a normal, liquor-free life.

I do not want to make this seem to be simple. It is not. I would prefer to see an alcoholic take the whole training and thus become submerged in a holistic approach to this complicated holistic problem. But many can conquer this problem in the way described. Begin today.

Mental Imagery in Nonobjective Situations

It is easier to picture a kidney stone that you may never have seen than to picture the alcoholism that you may have continuously experienced. Still, we use the same programming procedure—the three-pictures-to-the-left technique—for alcoholism that we use for the kidney stone. The picture of alcoholism might be a picture of the blood system saturated with alcohol, or it might be a picture of an unhealthy liver. But the easiest image to picture is one we have already seen with our eyes—ourselves staggering because of a spinning world or sitting at a bar emptying glass after glass.

This image identifies the problem. That is what you picture straight ahead. Then you move the picture slightly to the left and begin a correction to the problem. What do you picture now? The third and final picture will be a sober you and a stable world with no bar in sight. But how do you reach that point? What is the second picture?

No two alcoholics are alike. What works with one is not necessarily right for another. In the test described above, the alcoholics took the entire Silva training, which is devoted not just to the health applications discussed in this book but to the many other ways of enhancing the whole person not covered here.

Help With Smoking and Overeating

As the drinking habit can eventually sap our health and cause our demise, so can excessive behavior in other areas. It is a fact that you have a better chance of living longer as a nonsmoker than as a smoker.

Let us examine how you can use your alpha level to decrease or stop smoking. We will use the same basic procedures, but I am going to introduce here a triggering technique, similar to the Three-Fingers Technique. Simply defined, the triggering technique is programming that triggers a desired result whenever we do a simple specific action.

As you will recall, the Three-Fingers Technique triggered more of your mind to go to work for you.

Remember the priest I helped? I promised to explain why I had him drink water. Drinking the water was a triggering technique. I programmed that every time he sipped the water he would heal and get better and better. You can program that every time you take a drink of water your immediate desire to take a cigarette will disappear or your immediate desire to have a snack in between meals will disappear.

You can program that every time you take three deep breaths it will act in the same way for you—to remove the immediate desire to light up or go to the refrigerator.

There is more to it. Excessive smoking or excessive eating, like excessive drinking, is a problem of the whole person, so it needs a holistic solution. The ingredients of the solution are not the same for everyone, so the best I can do here is list a number of steps. Try them. Adopt whichever ones appear to work for you. The first two steps are the most important; they are a prerequisite to embarking on any of the others.

Smoking

1. Go to your alpha level and analyze your habit. When do you indulge? How do you feel at the time?
2. Give yourself daily programming to overcome the personality weakness detected in Step 1.
3. Adopt a triggering technique—for example, taking three deep breaths or drinking some water to end the immediate desire to smoke.
4. Use the three-picture technique. For smoking,
   Picture 1. You are a smoker.
   Picture 2. You are using your personality-strengthening and triggering techniques.
   Picture 3. You are a nonsmoker. There is a calendar on the wall showing the date (about one month from when you started).

5. Program that you will smoke later in the day or have longer intervals between cigarettes. Do this progressively as you reach each stage successfully.

Overeating

1. Go to your alpha level and analyze your habit. When do you indulge? How do you feel at the time?
2. Give yourself daily programming to overcome the personality weakness detected in Step 1.
3. Adopt a triggering technique such as deep breaths, drinking water, or eating a piece of carrot or celery to end the immediate desire to snack.
4. Use the three-picture technique. For overeating,
   Picture 1. Visualize yourself with the eating problem.
   Picture 2. You are using your personality-strengthening and triggering techniques.
   Picture 3. You are your proper weight. Imagine the scale. Imagine the calendar on the wall showing the date as you planned it. Imagine your clothing size the way it should be.
5. Program that fattening foods (fat, sugar, junk) no longer appeal to you and that the more nutritional foods satisfy you fully.

Session 27
Right-Brain Healing: Review

1. Close your eyes and roll them slightly upward toward your eyebrows.
2. Steps 2A, 3A, 3B, and 3C are optional. Count from 25 to 1. Count slowly and silently. Wait about one second between numbers.
   A. Starting with your scalp, focus your conscious attention on the different parts of your body from head to toe, relaxing them as you go.
3. When you reach the count of 1, hold a picture of yourself in your mind as youthful, radiant, healthy, and attractive.
   A. Ask yourself mentally, "Why do I have this physical problem?" Then let your mind wander.
   B. When you find yourself thinking about a certain person, picture that person.
   C. Picture yourself forgiving each other. Imagine a hug or a handshake, smiles, and heads nodding in agreement. Feel good about this.
4. Repeat mentally, "I will always maintain a perfectly healthy body and mind."
5. Say to yourself, "I am going to count from 1 to 5; when I reach the count of 5, I will open my eyes, feeling fine and in perfect health, feeling better than before."
6. Count. When you reach 3, repeat, "When I reach the count of 5, I will open my eyes, feeling fine and in perfect health, feeling better than before."
7. At the count of 5, open your eyes and affirm mentally, "I am wide awake, feeling fine and in perfect health, feeling better than before. And this is so."

The Versatile Right Hemisphere

Whatever you do with the right hemisphere seems to work. It is a versatile organ. Because it is creative and not destructive, when you activate it, it creates solutions.

Music can heal.

Art can heal.

Laughter can heal.

Love can heal.

Imagination can heal.

That is because they are right-brain activators.

The Silva Method is just one way to use the brain's right hemisphere to do its creative healing work. It gives you a simple methodology to use visualization and imagination to heal. And it works. Even with the Silva Method, the right brain is versatile. You can deviate from the specific steps and still gain benefits. The components are the alpha level and the desire, belief, and expectation for healing.

The Basic Silva Healing Procedure

1. Visualize yourself in a mental picture directly in front of you, identifying the health problem (one to two minutes).
2. Move the mental picture slightly to the left and imagine corrective action taking place (about twelve minutes).
3. Move the mental picture again slightly to the left and imagine yourself free of the problem and in perfect health (one to two minutes).

Improving Visualization

Mental picturing is necessary, but sharp and detailed mental picturing, though preferable, is not necessary. Here are some tips:

1. To better visualize yourself, practice with a mirror. Memorize your face, close your eyes, and visualize your face; open your eyes to see how well you did. Repeat until you are satisfied.

2. To better visualize generally, practice during the day, stopping to visualize or imagine objects you read about or hear about.
3. If you have never seen the health problem because it is internal, imagine what it might look like and trust your imagination.

Here is an example to help improve visualization:

Visualization and Imagination to Help a Heart Vessel Problem

1. Go to alpha.
2. Visualize yourself straight ahead with the heart problem. Use a typical scene in which you might experience chest pains.
3. Move the picture slightly to the left and imagine a correction taking place. The plaque inside the heart's blood vessels is being cleaned out or dissolved.
4. Move the picture again slightly to the left and imagine yourself perfect. You might use the same picture as in Step 2, but now you have no chest pains.
5. End your alpha session.
6. Repeat three times daily.

Quick Reviews for Ending Destructive Habits

Below are three quick reviews on the procedures covered in the preceding chapter.

Working on Ego Strength for Alcoholism

1. Go to your alpha level and analyze your drinking habit.
2. In daily alpha-level sessions, give yourself positive affirmations to strengthen these personality weaknesses (insecurity, poor self-concept, etc.) that may have surfaced in Step 1.

3. Use the basic Silva healing procedure, outlined above. First, picture yourself intoxicated. Next, picture yourself responding to your ego-strengthening affirmations of Step 2 (repeating them). You are acquiring a new look. In the third picture, you are a nondrinker, looking and feeling great.

Ending the Smoking Habit

1. Go to your alpha level and analyze your smoking habit. When do you take a cigarette? How do you feel when you light up?
2. Give yourself alpha affirmations to overcome the personality quirks detected in Step 1.
3. Program at alpha that three deep breaths will stop the immediate desire to smoke.
4. Use the basic Silva healing procedure. In the first picture, you are a smoker. In the second picture, you are using Steps 2 and 3. In the third picture, you see a date about a month from your starting date and you are a nonsmoker.
5. Program that you will have your first cigarette later in the day and that the interval between cigarettes will be longer. Do this step by step.

Ending the Overeating Habit

1. Go to your alpha level and analyze your eating habit. When do you take your first between-meal snack? How do you feel?
2. Give yourself alpha affirmations to overcome the personality quirks detected in Step 1—for example, "Every day I become more and more confident in myself."
3. Program at alpha that some triggering technique will stop your immediate desire to snack—for example, three deep breaths, a slice of apple, a carrot stick.
4. Use the basic Silva healing procedure. In the first pic-

ture, you are overweight as now. In the second picture, you are practicing Steps 2 and 3. In the third picture, you are slim; note your clothing size and the date on the calendar.

5. Program that fattening foods (fats, sweets, junk) no longer appeal to you and that the more nutritional foods satisfy you fully.

Using "Mental Movies" to Heal

Use an alternative procedure to the basic Silva healing procedure when visualization of internal or mental problems is difficult:

1. Go to alpha.
2. Imagine that you are inside your body at the trouble spot if internal, or involved in some unwanted behavior if mental.
3. Roll the camera. See a mental movie in which the trouble is being improved. Fantasize total correction.
4. End your alpha session. Repeat three times daily.

Session 28
Helping Yourself by Helping Others

1. Close your eyes and roll them slightly upward toward your eyebrows.
2. Steps 2A, 3A, 3B, and 3C are optional. Count from 25 to 1. Count slowly and silently. Wait about one second between numbers.
   A. Starting with your scalp, focus your conscious awareness on the different parts of your body from head to toe, relaxing them as you go.
3. When you reach the count of 1, hold a picture of yourself in your mind as youthful, radiant, healthy, and attractive.
   A. Ask yourself mentally, "Why do I have this physical problem?" Then let your mind wander.
   B. When you find yourself thinking about a certain person, picture that person.
   C. Picture yourself forgiving each other. Imagine a hug or a handshake, smiles, and heads nodding in agreement. Feel good about this.
4. Repeat mentally, "I will always maintain a perfectly healthy body and mind."
5. Say to yourself, "I am going to count from 1 to 5; when I reach the count of 5, I will open my eyes, feeling fine and in perfect health, feeling better than before."
6. Count. When you reach 3, repeat, "When I reach the count of 5, I will open my eyes, feeling fine and in perfect health, feeling better than before."
7. At the count of 5, open your eyes and affirm mentally, "I am wide awake, feeling fine and in perfect health, feeling better than before. And this is so."

The scene is a home in a residential area outside of Honolulu, Hawaii. Some thirty Silva graduates and friends are attending a bimonthly get-together where they hear a guest speaker and then participate in a group healing session for the name that is offered. Edward E. Kenney of Thunder Bay, Ontario, Canada, who is currently attending the University of Hawaii, gives the name of his sister Colleen in Thunder Bay, who has been suffering for many years from Crohn's disease, a chronic inflammation of the small intestine. There is no known cure. When operated on, there is a 50 percent chance that the disease will spread.

Five years earlier, Colleen had had a portion of her small intestine removed, but the disease continued to spread. She suffered periodic Crohn's disease attacks, which have the severity of an appendicitis attack. She was in and out of hospitals. Now she was ready for another surgery attempt.

"Colleen Marie Kenney, thirty-one years old, living in Rossport, Ontario, Canada, Crohn's disease" was all that Kenney told those present. They went to their alpha levels, deepened their levels, silently prayed for a moment, and then each in an individual way "fixed up" Colleen. In less than three minutes they were given another person to work on.

A few weeks later, Colleen traveled to Honolulu to visit her brother. "You know what, Ed?" she said one day in their Waikiki apartment. "I don't have Crohn's disease anymore." Ed Kenney looked at her and smiled. "I just have this feeling that the Crohn's is gone," she went on. "I just know it. I know it's gone!"

He then explained to her about the Silva meeting. "Would you like to share your feelings with them at their next meeting?" Colleen agreed.

A few days later, members of the group were treated to living proof of their power—a universal power to which we all have access.

A year later, Kenney wrote to us in Laredo of this case, bringing us up to date: "My sister remains in excellent health. Prior to this she was never able to work and relied on government assistance. This past year, she worked full-time outdoors during severe winter conditions at a provincial park. She was just recently hired as comanager of a new hotel."

Healings at a distance are commonplace among Silva Method graduates. It is more usual for an individual to help another person than it is for a group, as in the Kenney case, and of course the ailments eradicated are usually more common.

When you have mastered the alpha level, you too will be able to use your mind to help others heal, even at great distances. It might even be said that helping to heal another person is easier than healing oneself. Healing oneself is, in a way, like being a criminal and rectifying one's own crime. When you help another, you are at least starting from a neutral position. We use the same basic formula, but we do not have to spend as much time. Healing ourselves takes fifteen minutes a session. Healing another person takes three minutes a session and fewer sessions are necessary.

But one more difficult factor enters the picture: science is only at the very beginning of understanding this sort of healing, so the logic of the process is not fully within our grasp. My mind runs my body, so I can make myself sick and well. But what has my mind got to do with *your* body? That question can well serve as a stumbling block to your logical left brain, and it can block your right brain's work with its insistence, "I can't."

Of course, after you succeed in healing another, you know you can do it. Still, to begin, it will be useful to have a logical, though necessarily unconfirmed explanation of why you can do it.

So here goes.

Take the case of Marge Wolcott of Port Isabel, Texas. She used the Silva Method to help others and in the process she helped rid herself of a crippling disease:

I had multiple sclerosis (MS) for fifteen years. When I came to the Silva Method lectures, I was wearing a body brace and neck brace. I had to bring a special chair to sit in. I had strong faith, but it was doubled after I finished the Basic Lecture Series.

Two months after graduating, in March 1970, I took the neck brace off. Two months later, in May, the body brace broke across the back, the shoulder area. My daughter, who had taken the Silva Method training with me, suggested I quit wearing it. She knew I had been tempted to take it off.

I tried it, and have not worn it since. In fact, later a doctor from Dallas who had a crippling illness and had to close his practice came to visit me. I didn't know it then, but he knew a lot about MS, and said later he could not detect any signs that I'd ever had it! I heard that he took the Silva Method training, recovered, and reopened his practice.

After I recovered from MS, I saw my doctor again. His only comment was that he's heard of this kind of thing happening, but this was the first time he had ever seen it. He had felt there was no hope of my recovering. I had worn the braces for about seven or eight years.

Here's what I did: using the Silva Method, I programmed three times a day. Many people were calling me, asking me to help them, so I would go to level three times a day to program for them. Since I was programming for them, I'd also program for myself after I had finished programming for them.

I knew the doctors felt there was no hope for me, so I had little hope for myself. I had desire, of course, and I would not have bothered programming if I had not had some expectation that it would help. But I was not concerned about it. If I got better, that would be great. If not, I could accept that.

The Bible says that whatever you do for others comes back to you tenfold. Apparently when I programmed for other people I was helping myself, too. The thoughts of healing seemed to have influenced my own brain to make corrections in my body. It has been twelve years since I graduated from the Silva Method, and I have had no trouble since then with the MS.

One of the challenges I had at that time was severe pain in my face, the face muscles. When I heard about the Headache-Control Technique [given later in the book], it felt like someone had placed a hand on my shoulder. The pain in my face stopped and has not returned since.

How much of Marge's healing was due to her work on herself and how much to her work on other people is impossible to say. At the alpha level—the level of oneness—the distinction between self and others becomes blurred, if indeed it exists at all.

The right hemisphere appears to be our connection to the source of creation, the causal realm from which space, time, and a material world emerge into the physical, or effect, realm. In the causal realm, there is no space and time. How can there be separation, if there is no space?

Heal somebody else and you heal yourself.

Consider the act of helping others to heal a selfish act, one in which you are the chief beneficiary. You are helping all of humanity—and you are a paid-up member.

Session 29
Healing at a Distance

1. Close your eyes and roll them slightly upward toward your eyebrows.
2. Steps 2A, 3A, 3B, and 3C are optional. Count from 25 to 1. Count slowly and silently. Wait about one second between numbers.
   A. Starting with your scalp, focus your conscious awareness on the different parts of your body from head to toe, relaxing them as you go.
3. When you reach the count of 1, hold a picture of yourself in your mind as youthful, radiant, healthy, and attractive.
   A. Ask yourself mentally, "Why do I have this physical problem?" Then let your mind wander.
   B. When you find yourself thinking about a certain person, picture that person.
   C. Picture yourself forgiving each other. Imagine a hug or a handshake, smiles, and heads nodding in agreement. Feel good about this.
4. Repeat mentally, "I will always maintain a perfectly healthy body and mind."
5. Say to yourself, "I am going to count from 1 to 5; when I reach the count of 5, I will open my eyes, feeling fine and in perfect health, feeling better than before."
6. Count. When you reach 3, repeat, "When I reach the count of 5, I will open my eyes, feeling fine and in perfect health, feeling better than before."
7. At the count of 5, open your eyes and affirm mentally, "I am wide awake, feeling fine and in perfect health, feeling better than before. And this is so."

Five Case Histories

N.S. had gone through her second operation for malignancy in the intestines when her case was given to a Silva graduate. Working at the alpha level, the graduate used an imaginary laser light to cleanse the body of N.S. of all malignant cells. Months later, N.S. showed no trace of the problem. The distance between N.S. and the graduate was three thousand miles.

L.E. reported to a Silva graduate that his newborn son, four days old, had not had his first bowel movement. The hospital would not release the child until this took place, and if it did not occur in the next twenty-four hours, tests would have to be made.

"Can you help?" he asked the graduate.

"Call me back in ten minutes," was the reply.

The graduate went to alpha level, imagined that he saw the infant, pictured what the digestive system looked like, sensed a problem, and fixed it. A few minutes later, when L.E. called, the graduate reported what he had done. "The small intestine was fine, but where it meets the large intestine there was a closure like the neck of a new balloon. I blew it open. Everything should now be fine."

The next morning L.E.'s wife called from the hospital that the nurses reported the baby had had a "huge bowel movement" that night. L.E.'s wife and baby were leaving the hospital. The distance involved in this case was only two miles.

A New York couple was six thousand miles from home when they heard of a Silva graduate group. They asked the group to work on the wife's mother, who was suffering in the last stages of cancer. "She has been hanging by a thread for weeks." The next day, the wife called home. Her mother had passed away a few hours after the group's work. She called the group leader to thank the group.

"God's will has been done," she said.

Part of the Silva Method procedure when sending healing help is first to have a moment of prayer. Though not directed, that prayer is frequently, "God's will be done."

L.S. had a fast-mounting fever. She and her husband were visiting friends, who were holding a meeting to discuss the healing powers of the mind. L.S. was brought up as a case in point. The ten people present, all without training, decided to test their abilities to relax and mentally picture a correction taking place in L.S. By morning, L.S.'s fever had dropped from 104 degrees to normal. There was no large distance in this case. L.S. was in the adjoining room.

A Silva graduate decided to visit a friend in the hospital who was having a problem with his prostate gland. When he arrived in the hospital room late in the afternoon, his friend reported that he was supposed to be released the next day and that the tube to permit him to urinate had been removed, but although he had thought he had been emptying his bladder during the day, apparently he had not been. Now, he was in great distress. The nurse could not reach the doctor to get permission to put the tube back in. Tears rolled down his cheeks.

"I can't remember crying since I was a kid," he said, "but this is trouble."

The Silva graduate knew that it was possibly illegal for him to work on an ill person in that person's presence, but he would not walk out on his friend. So he defocused his eyes to go to level and imagined that he was applying a pain reliever to the bladder and stretching its capacity.

When he refocused his eyes, his friend was resting as if he was half asleep. Shortly, the nurse arrived. She had finally reached the doctor and had received permission to replace the tube. Distance involved in this case: ten feet.

Ten feet to ten thousand miles, your mind functions in healing ways. Distance is no limiting factor.

Session 30
Energy Fields

1. Close your eyes and roll them slightly upward toward your eyebrows.
2. Steps 2A, 3A, 3B, and 3C are optional. Count from 25 to 1. Count slowly and silently. Wait about one second between numbers.
   A. Starting with your scalp, focus your conscious awareness on the different parts of your body from head to toe, relaxing them as you go.
3. When you reach the count of 1, hold a picture of yourself in your mind as youthful, radiant, healthy, and attractive.
   A. Ask yourself mentally, "Why do I have this physical problem?" Then let your mind wander.
   B. When you find yourself thinking about a certain person, picture that person.
   C. Picture yourself forgiving each other. Imagine a hug or a handshake, smiles, and heads nodding in agreement. Feel good about this.
4. Repeat mentally, "I will always maintain a perfectly healthy body and mind."
5. Say to yourself, "I am going to count from 1 to 5; when I reach the count of 5, I will open my eyes, feeling fine and in perfect health, feeling better than before."
6. Count. When you reach 3, repeat, "When I reach the count of 5, I will open my eyes, feeling fine and in perfect health, feeling better than before."
7. At the count of 5, open your eyes and affirm mentally, "I am wide awake, feeling fine and in perfect health, feeling better than before. And this is so."

Because the universe is energy and not simply solid physical matter, we can affect people at great distances.

Even what we consider to be the solid material universe is energy. Consciousness is energy. Human beings are energy, and with training we can perceive the shape and significance of this energy. And we can effect changes in this energy.

I have already mentioned the human aura and how it can be photographed with Kirlian photography. Actually, this is only a portion of the energy fields that emanate from and/or surround the human body and consciousness. Energy fields can be at many levels. Electrical energy, for instance, can be D.C. or A.C., sixty cycles or faster or slower. It is still electricity.

Electricity is objective energy. It is electrons in motion in unison. It can be detected and measured. As you move from electrical energy to the energies of consciousness and life, you move through objective energies into subjective energies. You might say that subjective energies are more "rarified." They are less physical and more spiritual. They are closer to the primal energy of creation itself. We human beings radiate both objective and subjective energies.

The objective energy fields are believed to radiate no less than twenty-five feet in all directions from the human body. The distance at which this energy can be detected, of course, depends on the sensitivity of the detecting instruments. These include such instruments as infrared detectors, which detect part of the human aura radiation that can be felt, and infrared photographic equipment, which detects what can be seen.

The objective body radiation is limited by distance but the subjective part of the body radiation is not limited by distance. Some people can detect a part of the objective body radiation with their naked eyes. People who can see human-body radiation are known as aura readers. Their sense of sight can perceive the low end of the visual spectrum, around seven thousand angstroms. Some of these individuals have developed the ability to detect people's psychological or physiological problems through aura reading.

Before the Silva Method was developed, I trained people to read auras so they would be aware of people's problems, but this required that the person with the problem be present. After I developed the Silva Method, I stopped training aura readers, because with the use of the Silva Method techniques, a clairvoyant can detect a person's problems whether the problems are psychological or physiological, and whether the person is present or not present. In fact, clairvoyants trained with the Silva Method can detect people's problems no matter where those people happen to be.

Auras of the human body are said to be composed of seven radiating "dimensions," each connected to a source that is spiritual, in the sense that it is nonphysical. The point where each dimension connects to the physical is called a *chakra,* a Sanskrit word. There are seven centers of life energy in the human body counting from a chakra at the base of the spine to one at the top of the head.

Half of the seven radiating dimensions are physical and are in the visible world of the body. The other half are spiritual, in the invisible world of the mind (these are believed to be controlled by the right hemisphere). The first is the purely spiritual, subjective, immaterial energy field. The second is the subatomic energy field. The third is the atomic energy field. The fourth, the molecular energy field, is half physical and half spiritual, controlled by both brain hemispheres. The fifth, sixth, and seventh are the visible world of the body and include the cellular energy field, the single-organ energy field, and the organ-system energy field (such as the circulatory, respiratory, or digestive system). These are believed to be controlled by the left-brain hemisphere.

Each energy field radiates differently in different people. The radiation of each energy field is the composite, the sum total of effects of many variables, such as the line of ancestors of an individual and the transmission of genes, chromosomes, and both objective and subjective body radiation from the father and mother to the offspring.

The physical energy fields controlled by the left-brain hemisphere are limited by distance, as are the spiritual energy fields controlled by the left-brain hemisphere. But the spiritual energy fields controlled by the right-brain hemisphere are not limited by distance. These are the energy fields we activate when we help heal others at a distance.

The way the physical energy fields work is the reverse of the way spiritual energy fields work. The physical energy fields influence matter by repulsion, from the outer to the inner levels of matter. The spiritual energy fields influence matter by attraction, from the inner to the outer levels of matter. Mind, controlled by human intelligence at the alpha level, can influence all of these energy fields through either the left- or right-brain hemisphere.

Visualizing and imagining at this alpha level alters brain function, which in turn alters the body-energy radiation called the aura.

The nature of this alteration depends on the psychological and physiological state of the person transmitting the energy. All that is needed is your sincere desire to help another person correct a health abnormality and the expectation and belief that your mental image held at alpha level is real energy doing real work. And it is so.

Setting Up Right-Brain Points of Reference

In the second half of the thirty-two-hour Silva Method training, to help students work better with people at a distance we go through a process that activates the right-brain hemisphere. This process establishes points of reference in the right hemisphere similar to those we have been constantly establishing in the left hemisphere.

In its orientation to the physical world, the left brain has been endowed with thousands of points of reference. These points begin to be established on day one when the infant sees different faces and continues on subsequent days as the infant experiences different tastes, sounds, smells, and touch sensations. It goes on throughout adulthood, as the individual experiences new places, new people, new shows, new restaurants, new clothing, new education, and new activities. These are all new left-brain, physical-world points of reference.

But with a few exceptions, such as music and art, the right brain is left out. We do not educate the right hemisphere. It is like a wasteland, with no street signs, no signposts, no points of reference. It is this situation that we rectify in the second half of the Silva Method training. We endow the right hemisphere with points of reference. In the eight mind-training cycles, each taking close to half an hour, the Silva lecturer leads students through mental-picturing exercises that establish hundreds of points of reference in the right-brain hemisphere at all levels of matter, from the inanimate to the human level. It is not possible to accomplish this in an equally effective way in the pages of a book.

Still, you will be able to help others. You have a right-brain hemisphere. As you help yourself and then begin to help others, you will be setting up right-brain points of reference. What was in effect a wasteland will begin to develop points of reference through the feedback you gain through practice. The more you practice helping yourself and helping others, the more right-brain points of reference you will acquire and the better you will be at using them.

Just as it has taken more time for your morning countdown to put you in control of your alpha level, so you will need more time to gain more and more control of the good health of others. But you will get there.

The Nature of Psychic or Clairvoyant Ability

Let me take you inside a Silva training classroom during the final hours. The students are in groups of three. They are taking turns doing cases. A case is a person who is quite sick or in trouble.

The student who knows this sick person has written the individual's name, address, age, and sex on a piece of paper. On the back of the paper is noted the illness or illnesses and a description of the person such as you might find on a driver's license. The contact then asks another student to go to alpha level.

The contact student presenting the case is called the orientologist. The student who works the case is called the psychorientologist, or psychic for short. The third student notes down everything the psychic says, and this information is reviewed later to help the psychic establish points of reference.

When the pychic reaches alpha level he or she says, "I'm ready."

The orientologist then gives the name, address, age, and sex of the sick person, the person the psychic does not know. The psychic then scans the body to detect the illness and relates the findings to the orientologist. The psychic then corrects the problems detected in the sick person, using the standard positive mental-imagining procedure, and ends the alpha session. Then they discuss the case.

The orientologist is always flabbergasted at the accuracy of the psychic's findings, but when the roles are reversed, the orientologist is able to demonstrate that same level of accuracy, which usually averages 80 percent among Silva students.

You will be able to be just as accurate when you work on your own with my help through this book and with practice. The Silva Method brings out abilities that are dormant within all of us. You are a psychic. You can detect information at a distance. You can heal at a distance.

Session 31
The Procedure for Remote Healing

1. Close your eyes and roll them slightly upward toward your eyebrows.
2. Steps 2A, 3A, 3B, and 3C are optional. You are now ready to reduce your count from 25 to 1 to 10 to 1. Count slowly and silently. Wait about one second between numbers.
   A. Starting with your scalp, focus your conscious awareness on the different parts of your body from head to toe, relaxing them as you go.
3. When you reach the count of 1, hold a picture of yourself in your mind as youthful, radiant, healthy, and attractive.
   A. Ask yourself mentally, "Why do I have this physical problem?" Then let your mind wander.
   B. When you find yourself thinking about a certain person, picture that person.
   C. Picture yourself forgiving each other. Imagine a hug or a handshake, smiles, and heads nodding in agreement. Feel good about this.
4. Repeat mentally, "I will always maintain a perfectly healthy body and mind."
5. Say to yourself, "I am going to count from 1 to 5; when I reach the count of 5, I will open my eyes, feeling fine and in perfect health, feeling better than before."
6. Count. When you reach 3, repeat, "When I reach the count of 5, I will open my eyes, feeling fine and in perfect health, feeling better than before."
7. At the count of 5, open your eyes and affirm mentally, "I am wide awake, feeling fine and in perfect health, feeling better than before. And this is so."

Imagine that a friend of yours, knowing of your work with the Silva Method, approaches and asks if you can help him with a health problem.

"Surely," you reply graciously. "What's the problem?"

"Guess," says he.

An outrageous reply. It will probably never happen—but in a way it happens every time.

"My back keeps conking out," may be his reply, but he is really saying, "Guess."

Or his reply may be, "My doctor says I have arthritis." Again, translate that answer into, "Guess."

Health problems are not always what they are said to be or initially appear to be. Medical diagnosis is an art as well as a science. The person with a pain in the pit of the stomach may have a hernia problem several inches below the pained area. Different health problems often cause identical symptoms.

The only way to know for sure what the problem really is is to get your information directly from "the horse's mouth," through clairvoyant detection. Your right-brain hemisphere knows how to do this. All you have to do is desire to know the nature of the problem, have a desire to correct it, and activate the hemisphere.

Let's boil that down into a step-by-step how-to:

1. You go to alpha level, deepen it with another countdown, and say a brief prayer.
2. In your desire to identify the problem, scan the body up and down, thinking of possible problems and expecting to have your attention called to the problem area.
3. When your awareness is attracted to a part of the body, proceed with your healing as before.

Step 2 feels like guessing. After all, there is no objective sensory input to lead you to a conclusion, and for most of your life you have been taught that objective sensory input is the only way to go, that everything else is guessing. Those who taught you this approach are left-brain people. Do not think any less of them. They too learned from left-brain teachers.

How to Heal Others at a Distance

You already know the procedure to heal yourself. You use the same procedure to help others at a distance:

1. Go to alpha.
2. Use the three pictures.
   Picture 1. Visualize the problem.
   Picture 2. Imagine the healing taking place.
   Picture 3. Imagine the problem healed.
3. End your session.

However, some additional factors and variations come into play with remote healing. Healing others requires a deeper level of mind than healing yourself. So it is best to use an additional countdown of 10 to 1 after your 5 to 1 (when you have reached that level). A deeper level of mind is a more creative level, so the deeper you go the greater is your ability to make corrections in abnormalities.

I have delayed giving you the method for healing others at a distance to allow you more time to practice relaxation, visualization, and imagination.

The novice in relaxation, visualization, and imagination has not acquired the self-assuredness necessary to permit expectation and belief to power mental work. When you have attained positive feedback working on yourself, you are primed for working on others. This priming is taking place through the medium of these pages, too, but there is no substitute for practice leading to successful results.

When you work on others, you need not spend fifteen minutes at your alpha level. Each of the three mental pictures requires only a minute or so of your time. However, there is an optimum time to work on another person. When you work on yourself, the best time to spend these fifteen minutes three times a day is upon waking in the morning, after lunch, and when you go to bed. At these times, you are most relaxed and open to right-brain functioning.

But you will not know the other person's schedule for arising, lunching, and retiring. So you need to program at night for optimum results. Even at night, however, the other person's brain waves will be busy doing their work. There are optimum and poor times to program. You already know how to solve this dilemma. Just before you go to sleep, program to awaken automatically at the best time to program the other person. Then, the first time you awaken during the night, go to your alpha level and proceed with your three mental pictures.

Combining these steps, here, then, is the three-scenes procedure for helping another person heal:

1. Go to your level before falling asleep and instruct yourself to awaken automatically at the best time to program the subject. Fall asleep from your level.
2. When you awaken during the night, use your 5 to 1 countdown to enter the alpha level. Then use an additional 10 to 1 countdown to deepen to a more creative level.
3. As you are now closer to the Creator, enjoy a moment of prayer or worshipful silence.
4. Visualize the subject directly in front of you. If you know the problem, mentally identify it visually; if you do not know the problem, imagine that you are detecting it, using the procedure on page 178. Spend one minute.
5. Move the mental picture slightly to the left and imagine the problem being corrected. Spend one or two minutes.
6. Move the mental picture again slightly to the left and imagine the subject free of the problem and in perfect health.
7. Fall asleep from your level.

It is best to program to wake up, as described, but of course it is possible to do your healing work during the day. If the health problem is a matter of life and death, however, or if the patient is not responding, then program to waken and repeat the healing at the best time at night.

Follow-Up Procedures

When we correct an abnormality subjectively at our level, we assume the patient is healing. However, if it is a life-or-death situation, we repeat the alpha session daily. Stubborn or chronic conditions that persist might require the healer to repeat the alpha session every three days. In such situations, it is best if the healer can get daily feedback. What change has occurred in the life-or-death situation? What change has occurred in a chronic ailment?

When you get feedback, you, as the healer, must change the first of the three mental pictures to conform with the changes that have taken place. When the patient knows of the healing and is willing to cooperate, you can inject a strengthening technique. To strengthen, use a reinforcing mechanism such as the drinking of water. Here is how:

1. Instruct the patient to fill a glass of water just before retiring and drink half the water, leaving the rest to drink first thing in the morning.
2. When healing at your alpha level, during the second mental picture imagine the patient drinking the water and getting better for doing so.

You are a left-brain/right-brain person. You have activated that part of your intelligence that is called intuition, gut feeling, or heightened perception. At deep alpha, you can "guess" in dependable ways. You can extend that guessing to business problems, critical decisions, human relationships, and other ways besides health to make this a better world to live in for yourself and others.

So the healing of others is more than correcting abnormalities. It is detecting them, also.

Session 32
Reinforcing Mechanisms to Help Healing

1. Close your eyes and roll them slightly upward toward your eyebrows.
2. Steps 2A, 3A, 3B, and 3C are optional. Count from 10 to 1.
   A. Starting with your scalp, focus your conscious awareness on the different parts of your body from head to toe, relaxing them as you go.
3. When you reach the count of 1, hold a picture of yourself in your mind as youthful, radiant, healthy, and attractive.
   A. Ask yourself mentally, "Why do I have this physical problem?" Then let your mind wander.
   B. When you find yourself thinking about a certain person, picture that person.
   C. Picture yourself forgiving each other. Imagine a hug or a handshake, smiles, and heads nodding in agreement. Feel good about this.
4. Repeat mentally, "I will always maintain a perfectly healthy body and mind."
5. Say to yourself, "I am going to count from 1 to 5; when I reach the count of 5, I will open my eyes, feeling fine and in perfect health, feeling better than before."
6. Count. When you reach 3, repeat, "When I reach the count of 5, I will open my eyes, feeling fine and in perfect health, feeling better than before."
7. At the count of 5, open your eyes and affirm mentally, "I am wide awake, feeling fine and in perfect health, feeling better than before. And this is so."

Advanced Healing Procedures Using Confusion

One advanced method of healing, which I identify as Healing Method No. 3-C, is to be used in the patient's presence. Owing to possible illegality in your state, it is best to limit its use to members of your family. It involves confusing the patient. When a person is confused, he or she accepts programming more readily. The confusion is brought about easily in conversation. The conversation might go like this: "It rained yesterday. But if the sun had not shone so brightly I would not have gotten wet. Maybe the weather will be better the day before yesterday. I perspire so when it's cold."

Any totally illogical talk will quickly confuse the patient sufficiently for effective programming. After the healing has confused the patient, then from level the healer uses the three-pictures technique, including a reinforcing mechanism if desired to correct the patient's problem. The most popular reinforcing mechanism is the glass of water, described in the preceding chapter.

To use this technique, the healer must have had practice in going into level with eyes open and vision defocused. When the patient is confused, the healer, with eyes open and defocused, visualizes the patient in front of the healer with the problem, and then in the second picture, imagines the patient drinking the water and getting better. The healer then imagines the patient in perfect health.

The healer then instructs the patient to drink the water in order for the healing treatment to work. The healer may continue the conversation and confuse the patient again in order to repeat the programming for reinforcement. If the patient begins to ask questions to remove the confusion, request that the patient not ask questions until the end of the session.

Expectation Method

Healing Method No. 4-E makes use of a state of expectation,

rather than a state of confusion, in the patient. The difference between Healing Method 3-C and Method 4-E is that in 3-C the healer confuses the patient in conversation and programs the patient while he or she is confused whereas in Method 4-E the healer creates a state of expectation in the patient and then mentally programs the patient while he or she is in that state of expectation.

To create a state of expectation, the healer speaks about something highly interesting. At the very point of highest interest, the healer pauses, leaving the patient in a state of high expectation. At that point, the healer defocuses the eyes and uses the three-scenes technique as in the other healing methods.

Using the Survival Mechanism

In Healing Method No. 5-ESM, the healer excites the patient's survival mechanism. When a patient's survival mechanism is excited, he or she can be programmed mentally by a healer who knows how to use the clairvoyant level and how to use the three scenes. The survival mechanism is excited when the subject is frightened; suffering an injury; punctured, as in acupuncture or with the injection of medicine; or even, for some, exposed to the sight of blood.

Healing Method No. 6-SBA works when the healer is able to slow down the patient's brain activity. With the brain activity slowed, a person can be programmed objectively and subjectively. A special type of relaxation exercise is taught in the advanced Silva Method training to slow a subject's brain activity.

If a patient does not react to your healing efforts, you may have to add a reinforcing mechanism or, if you already have programmed one, to change it. You will be having healing sessions for the patient nightly if it is a life-or-death case, every seventy-two hours for less critical cases. If no improvement is evident after three such sessions, the healer should look to the reinforcement mechanism. Add one to your procedure if there is none being used or change the one you have from, say, the glass of water to some other food or liquid that the patient uses more than once a day. I have seen a switch from a glass of water to a cup of tea, if that is what the patient takes, make a world of difference.

Helping Others Break Habits and Change Destructive Attitudes

For correcting health problems, anything the patient eats or drinks more than once a day can serve as a correcting-by-reinforcing mechanism. But correcting any other kind of problem, including unhealthful habits, can be very difficult if the person with the habit does not cooperate. Select any action or function the subject performs more than once a day—for example, "lighting up," reading a newspaper, or even walking.

When programming to correct a habit in a person, you will program not for the person to stop the habit, but for the person to enhance the desire to end the habit. When the person strongly wants to break the habit, he or she will seek help. This desire will make it easier to correct the problem, because the person will be willing to cooperate (for a detailed discussion of motivating others, see Chapter 42, which covers motivation and subjective communication to correct abnormal behavior).

When you are correcting an emotional or mental problem, visualize how the person acts with the problem in the first scene. Then, in the second scene, imagine the patient performing the selected reinforcement mechanism and imagine the problem being reduced. Finally, in the third scene, imagine the person without the problem, functioning normally.

A Review of the Procedures for Helping to Heal Others

Use these reviews as quick reference guides for healing others.

The Basic Procedure

Use this procedure only when you have practiced the count-down exercises for forty mornings to acquire the ability to go to the alpha level and only after you have used the alpha level successfully to help yourself. You can then help others using the same basic procedure that you used to help yourself.

1. Go to alpha.
2. Visualize the first picture and imagine the other two, moving them successively to the left—the person and the illness, the correction of the illness, and the person free from illness.
3. End your alpha session.

The Detailed Procedure

When healing others, some details in the basic procedure are added or changed:

1. Go to your alpha level at night and program to wake up automatically at the optimum time to program the subject.
2. When you awaken, go to alpha; then deepen your alpha level with an extra 10 to 1 countdown.
3. Before beginning to visualize the first picture, enjoy a moment of prayer.
4. Visualize the subject with the health problem. (If you do not know the problem, see below for the procedure to detect it.) Spend one minute.
5. Move the picture slightly to the left. Spend one or two minutes imagining the problem being corrected.
6. Move the picture slightly to the left again and imagine the subject free of the problem and in perfect health.

Detecting a Health Problem in Another Person

1. Go to alpha, deepen it, and say a brief prayer.
2. Ask yourself, "Where is the problem?" Then scan the body up and down until your attention is attracted to an area.
3. Assume that this is correct and proceed with your healing work as above.

Follow-Up Steps

- In a life-or-death situation, repeat your healing work every night. If the situation is not serious, repeat every three days.
- In a serious situation or one that does not immediately respond, use reinforcing mechanisms such as the drinking of a glass of water. Program the subject that each drink helps the healing.
- If the subject does not respond even with the reinforcing mechanism, change the reinforcing mechanism from drinking water to eating food or drinking tea or coffee, something that the subject is known to do more than once daily.
- With each forward step as the healing progresses, change the negative mental picture to the new improved condition.

Helping Others Break Habits and Change Destructive Thoughts

Program a reinforcing mechanism—some common action the subject is known to perform more than once a day. Then go through the same procedure as for an illness, but with these exceptions:

1. Your three pictures should not be of the habit disappearing but of the subject wanting strongly to break the habit.

2. Subjects with emotional problems or mental problems can be helped by the standard three-scenes procedure. Imagine these scenes:

   Picture 1. The subject functioning abnormally.
   Picture 2. The abnormality being corrected.
   Picture 3. The subject free of the emotional or mental problem.

Session 33
Subjective Communication

1. Close your eyes and roll them slightly upward toward your eyebrows.
2. Steps 2A, 3A, 3B, and 3C are optional. Count from 10 to 1.
   A. Starting with your scalp, focus your conscious awareness on the different parts of your body from head to toe, relaxing them as you go.
3. When you reach the count of 1, hold a picture of yourself in your mind as youthful, radiant, healthy, and attractive.
   A. Ask yourself mentally, "Why do I have this physical problem?" Then let your mind wander.
   B. When you find yourself thinking about a certain person, picture that person.
   C. Picture yourself forgiving each other. Imagine a hug or a handshake, smiles, and heads nodding in agreement. Feel good about this.
4. Repeat mentally, "I will always maintain a perfectly healthy body and mind."
5. Say to yourself, "I am going to count from 1 to 5; when I reach the count of 5, I will open my eyes, feeling fine and in perfect health, feeling better than before."
6. Count. When you reach 3, repeat, "When I reach the count of 5, I will open my eyes, feeling fine and in perfect health, feeling better than before."
7. At the count of 5, open your eyes and affirm mentally, "I am wide awake, feeling fine and in perfect health, feeling better than before. And this is so."

Subjective Communication

One of the most important findings to emerge from right-brain/left-brain research is that the right brain functions in a spaceless, timeless realm. The timelessness is shocking enough, but spacelessness is nearly beyond imagining.

The right brain's ability to function as if space did not exist makes you and me more than members of the human family. It makes us one. If there is no separation in the right-brain, or causal, realm, then we all share the same causal source. Our separate bodies may not be connected in the objective physical realm, but our seemingly separate minds are indeed connected in the subjective, nonphysical realm.

I have shown you how the Silva Method uses that connection to enable us to heal sickness in others. Here I want to focus on using that connection to heal other kinds of abnormalities in others.

Consider Mrs. J.T.'s daughter, who had been married for one year. In that year she had made new friends—but of the wrong kind. She had drifted farther and farther away from the family into a fast crowd to which her new husband belonged. Nothing Mrs. J.T. said to her daughter helped. In fact, her words only served to widen the breach between them. It was at this time that Mrs. J.T. took the Silva Method training. She used it immediately on her daughter's problem.

She went to alpha level. She had an imaginary conversation with her daughter. She ended her session. The next morning she decided to visit her daughter. When her daughter opened the front door, she threw her arms around her mother, hugging her for the first time in months. It was the start of an improved life-style for her daughter.

The Power of Subjective Words

How did that imaginary conversation at alpha "get through"? What was said?

Let us review several of the differences in left-brain and right-brain functioning as revealed by recent research at leading institutions. Much of this research was done with the help of an anesthetic, usually amelobarbitone, which "knocks out" the left or right brain, depending on which artery it is injected into.

By observing the behavior of people in whom one or the other of the brain hemispheres has been deactivated, researchers have been able to establish "job descriptions" for these two hemispheres. Let us examine three contrasting characteristics.

1. The left brain thrives on the material world, the senses, the physical. The right brain is oriented to the world of thought, feeling, perception.
2. The left brain thrives on detail, the nitty gritty, the ant's eye view. The right brain cannot tolerate detail. It sees, instead, the whole picture, the bird's eye view.
3. The left brain thrives on dichotomy, polarity, and conflict. It sees differences. The right brain overlooks differences to see instead "sameness." It sees common denominators. It sees the oneness.

Many more attributes of each hemisphere contribute to our immense human intelligence. But these three in particular need special emphasis. In fact, these three ways of thinking are the requirements for successful subjective communication.

The first mandates that we turn off the physical world and go to the world of the imagination—alpha. The second mandates that we see all people as one, that we rise above earthly differences and see each individual as a sort of Higher Self joined with our own Higher Self. The third mandates that we abandon the dichotomy of "I am right, you are wrong" and instead communicate "What is right"—a mutual solution. These three brain functions seem simple enough, but they are actually the exact reverse of our usual learned approaches to communication.

It takes a keen awareness of these three ways of thinking during an imaginary conversation to maintain right-brain participation. Without right-brain participation, the message does not get through.

Successfully Contacting Other Minds

Let us take a typical example.

Your three-year-old is still wetting the bed. No amount of talking to the child has helped. You decide to use subjective communication. You go to your alpha level. You visualize the child.

You mentally say, "You lousy brat! The next time you wet your bed, I'm going to rub your face in it!"

Does it work? No way. You broke all three rules. All you did correctly was to go to your alpha level, but even here you probably came up toward beta again as you expressed your unrelaxed irritation. The moment you said "lousy brat" you broke the connection. You created a superior-inferior relationship, which is bound to "turn off" the right brain.

Finally, by invoking a punishment, with you the punisher and the child as the punished, you chose separation, a left-brain characteristic. At this point, the right brain would bow out. Thinking at the alpha level must be creative, not destructive. For subjective communication to work, we must accept the other person as an equal. Subjective solutions offered must be material solutions that benefit both sender and receiver.

Another rule for subjective communication is to avoid a lot of details. Details are the "stuff" of the left brain. Keep the mutual solution simple, free of ifs, ands, and buts.

When you meet these basic requirements, you might handle the bed-wetting situation this way.

You go to your alpha level. You visualize the child. You mentally say, "Darling, wouldn't it be better, when you have to urinate, if you got up and went to the bathroom? You would have a more comfortable bed. You would sleep better. And I would not have to launder the sheets."

Simple. Together. Mutual. And effective.

Session 34
Centering and Health

1. Close your eyes and roll them slightly upward toward your eyebrows.
2. Steps 2A, 3A, 3B, and 3C are optional. Count from 10 to 1.
   A. Starting with your scalp, focus your conscious awareness on the different parts of your body from head to toe, relaxing them as you go.
3. When you reach the count of 1, hold a picture of yourself in your mind as youthful, radiant, healthy, and attractive.
   A. Ask yourself mentally, "Why do I have this physical problem?" Then let your mind wander.
   B. When you find yourself thinking about a certain person, picture that person.
   C. Picture yourself forgiving each other. Imagine a hug or a handshake, smiles, and heads nodding in agreement. Feel good about this.
4. Repeat mentally, "I will always maintain a perfectly healthy body and mind."
5. Say to yourself, "I am going to count from 1 to 5; when I reach the count of 5, I will open my eyes, feeling fine and in perfect health, feeling better than before."
6. Count. When you reach 3, repeat, "When I reach the count of 5, I will open my eyes, feeling fine and in perfect health, feeling better than before."
7. At the count of 5, open your eyes and affirm mentally, "I am wide awake, feeling fine and in perfect health, feeling better than before. And this is so."

Centering

The invention of the wheel was one of the great strides made by humanity in its climb from the primitive to the civilized life.

But we are still inventing the wheel.

People are still learning to be centered like the wheel. If the hub of the wheel is not exactly centered, it will not work smoothly as a wheel should. The motion will be hobbled. We say, then, that it is eccentric.

People who are not centered are eccentric. They do not roll smoothly along the road of life. They suffer from off-balance behavior. Their thinking is erratic. They swerve easily. They can be creative or destructive. Centered thinking is alpha thinking. Alpha is at the center of the human brain-wave frequency spectrum.

Scientists have discovered that the space between the planet earth and the ionosphere high above it forms a resonating cavity that contains electromagnetic energy vibrating at a frequency of ten cycles per second—the middle of the alpha range of human brain frequencies. Scientists suspect that the generator of these vibrations could be somewhere in the depths of the universe. But might the frequency be the average frequency of billions of human brains pulsating on earth below?

A centered person has more alpha frequencies than an eccentric one. You can recognize a centered person, because that person is more human—that is, more *humane*. Being more human also means being healthier and more spiritual. These improvements occur automatically as a person becomes centered by doing more thinking at the center of the brain-wave spectrum—that is, at the ten-cycle alpha dimension, which is the same frequency of the electromagnetic energy circling the planet earth.

As your thinking becomes more centered, first by using the morning countdown exercises to go to alpha, then by helping yourself to better health, and finally by going on to help others to better health, you become more human, a better person.

Your immune system becomes more alive. Your reproductive system becomes more alive. Your creative mind becomes more alive. Your intuition becomes more alive. And so you become a healthier, more attractive, more resourceful, and more successful person.

You also become a safer person, in tune with the flow of things. You are less likely to be involved in a traffic accident than an eccentric person, and less likely to create a reality with distortions, aberrations, and abnormalities.

Inner World, Outer World

Because this is a physical world and survival in it is paramount, we have naturally developed our logical, rational modes of thinking to a much greater degree than our modes of fantasizing and visualizing. We have given the outer world top priority over the inner world, and our preoccupation with that outer, physical world has eclipsed our inner-world skills to a large degree.

In the Silva Method, we beat the drums for the inner world. We do not propose to completely shift the emphasis and give the inner world priority over the outer world. But we do try for equality between inner and outer worlds. We work to activate the right hemisphere of the brain, our inner-world organ of intelligence, so that we use it as much as we use the left hemisphere of the brain, our outer-world organ of intelligence.

Some critics argue that the outer world is the *only* reality, and call the inner world unreal. They ignore the fact that all that is great in our history and culture has originated in the inner world.

An artist mentally sees a picture and then paints it. A composer mentally hears an entire composition and then merely puts it down on paper. The world's sacred spiritual scriptures have come to paper via the inner world of its scribes. Inventors have pictured their discoveries, physicists have dreamed their theories, and scientists have been rewarded with their findings through flashes of insight and intuition. The creative faculty of the human mind is our connection to the Creator. What our critics are really saying is: "It is wrong to be connected to God."

The real error would lie in breaking that connection. To do so would mean

- abandoning our power to create our own reality;
- abandoning our ability to handle stress, pain, and the spectrum of health conditions;
- abandoning our ability to dissolve negative thinking and substitute positive thinking in its place; and
- abandoning our creative, intuitive, and psychic abilities.

We have been created with a bicameral, or two-hemisphere, brain. But in a sense this is a house divided against itself, with the left brain "editing" the right brain and screening out most of its input.

By activating the right brain and demonstrating its ability to the dominant left brain, we acquire the benefits of our full brain working as a whole for more genius, health, and effectiveness. With both brain hemispheres working for you, you are centered—"in synch" with the universe.

Session 35
Using Deep Alpha

1. Close your eyes and roll them slightly upward toward your eyebrows.
2. Steps 2A, 3A, 3B, and 3C are optional. Count from 10 to 1.
   A. Starting with your scalp, focus your conscious awareness on the different parts of your body from head to toe, relaxing them as you go.
3. When you reach the count of 1, hold a picture of yourself in your mind as youthful, radiant, healthy, and attractive.
   A. Ask yourself mentally, "Why do I have this physical problem?" Then let your mind wander.
   B. When you find yourself thinking about a certain person, picture that person.
   C. Picture yourself forgiving each other. Imagine a hug or a handshake, smiles, and heads nodding in agreement. Feel good about this.
4. Repeat mentally, "I will always maintain a perfectly healthy body and mind."
5. Say to yourself, "I am going to count from 1 to 5; when I reach the count of 5, I will open my eyes, feeling fine and in perfect health, feeling better than before."
6. Count. When you reach 3, repeat, "When I reach the count of 5, I will open my eyes, feeling fine and in perfect health, feeling better than before."
7. At the count of 5, open your eyes and affirm mentally, "I am wide awake, feeling fine and in perfect health, feeling better than before. And this is so."

Deep Alpha Versus Shallow Alpha

You'll note that for some of the procedures described in this book, I have recommended going through an extra countdown to deepen the alpha level. I have not always recommended this extra countdown, even though it could be helpful in many cases. It has been in the reader's best interest to keep the procedures as short and as simple as possible.

A research project was recently conducted by a Silva Method lecturer at a local university. Eighteen Silva graduates participated. Ten went through an extra relaxation deepening process before going to alpha. Eight used only the standard method. All were then tested with their eyes open at alpha to measure their ability to visually detect and identify objects flashed for one-tenth of a second and to compare it with that ability at the beta level. The subjects who had deepened their alpha level with extra relaxation procedures identified fewer of the objects at alpha than at beta. On the other hand, the subjects who had entered alpha without the deepening procedures were able to identify more of the objects at alpha than they could at the beta level.

This experiment appears to confirm other research, and my own intuition, suggesting that people who go more deeply into alpha tend to temporarily set aside their cognitive controls and automatic sensory perceptions and gain in their place a more inwardly focused attention. A more shallow alpha increases outwardly based attention. Thus, a more shallow alpha is recommended for solving problems external to the body and mind—business problems, money problems, problems to do with material possessions. Deeper alpha, in which you use an extra countdown or progressive relaxation to take you to brain frequencies below ten cycles, diminishes awareness of exernal information but enhances the ability to maintain superior health.

The situation is not black or white. There is no rule involved. Go to alpha in any way you can when the need to help yourself or others arises. Defocus your eyes, if that is all you can do at the moment, and know that with the Silva Method that will suffice. Do the Three-Fingers Technique, if you have preprogrammed that technique, and it will suffice.

Count backward from whatever point you are in your forty-morning training countdown exercises. If you have completed your self-training, 5 to 1 will get you to a sufficiently deep level of alpha to do important health work for yourself and others. Add an extra 10 to 1 countdown and you will be at deeper alpha. At deeper alpha, you will be an even more effective healer of yourself and others.

I recommend deep alpha whenever possible for serious health problems. If this is not possible, for whatever reason, go to the deepest alpha you can reach. It will still be a healing level.

Session 36
Controlling Environmental Dangers

1. Close your eyes and roll them slightly upward toward your eyebrows.
2. Steps 2A, 3A, 3B, and 3C are optional. Count from 10 to 1.
   A. Starting with your scalp, focus your conscious awareness on the different parts of your body from head to toe, relaxing them as you go.
3. When you reach the count of 1, hold a picture of yourself in your mind as youthful, radiant, healthy, and attractive.
   A. Ask yourself mentally, "Why do I have this physical problem?" Then let your mind wander.
   B. When you find yourself thinking about a certain person, picture that person.
   C. Picture yourself forgiving each other. Imagine a hug or a handshake, smiles, and heads nodding in agreement. Feel good about this.
4. Repeat mentally, "I will always maintain a perfectly healthy body and mind."
5. Say to yourself, "I am going to count from 1 to 5; when I reach the count of 5, I will open my eyes, feeling fine and in perfect health, feeling better than before."
6. Count. When you reach 3, repeat, "When I reach the count of 5, I will open my eyes, feeling fine and in perfect health, feeling better than before."
7. At the count of 5, open your eyes and affirm mentally, "I am wide awake, feeling fine and in perfect health, feeling better than before. And this is so."

Nothing has yet been said on these pages about the effects of polluted air, water, or food on our health and how we might use the Silva Method to help detect and correct such problems. Now seems to be an appropriate point to consider this, as I have just talked about the enhanced ability at less deep levels of alpha to deal with the physical world. A word of caution first: negative thinking magnifies negative effects.

You might do more harm to yourself by worrying about the chemicals injected into chickens than by actually eating those chickens. You might do more harm to yourself by feeling guilty about ingesting all the sugar in that ice cream sundae than by actually eating the sugar. Worry and guilt mean stress. Stress can do harm more quickly than most environmental factors. It is preferable to use more of your mind to make sensible choices where options exist than to worry.

If you are at the supermarket and are wondering whether to buy the chopped beef or the pork chops, stop, defocus your eyes, and ask yourself, "Which is better for me at this time, chopped beef or pork chops?" Clear your mind, return to the job at hand—selecting one of the packages—and you will find yourself automatically moving your hand toward, say, the leaner chopped beef. If you have preprogammed the Three-Fingers Technique, keep your three fingers together while marketing. The more you have practiced the Silva Method, the more centered you will have become. As previously discussed, a centered person is more likely to make correct decisions.

Occasionally, the need for detecting poisons, irritants, or pollutants becomes more critical. Then it is best to go to alpha and follow a problem-solving procedure. Because this involves dealing with the physical world in the present, there is no need to deepen your alpha level.

Allergy

If you have a skin rash, indigestion, or some recurring allergic reaction, the wisest permanent approach is prevention, not just treatment of the symptom. You might begin by using the three pictures to heal the symptoms, but prevention should be the main goal. The best step for a permanent solution would be to detect what is causing the allergic reaction and then to avoid that food or substance.

Here, then, is the procedure.

1. Go to your alpha level and mentally picture yourself in front of you with the allergy. There is a calendar in view.
2. Ask yourself when and why the allergy started; turn the calendar slowly back, page by page, while slowly selecting pictures from the right (the past).
3. When a scene comes, permit it to be played out.
4. End your alpha session and analyze the memory that just surfaced. Understand it from today's perspective.

Understanding the event from today's perspective might very well end the allergy. If symptoms still persist, directing your programming to eliminate the symptoms is likely to end the problem without symptom substitution.

For a more detailed treatment of allergies, see Chapter 49.

Identifying the Cause of an Allergy

When the cause is one of several known foods or substances:

1. At alpha, visualize your physician or other respected authority standing in front of you.
2. Choose two foods or substances and ask your doctor which is more likely to be the cause of the allergy.
3. Come out of alpha and think about the problem; an answer will pop into your mind.
4. Compare that substance with another in the same way until one emerges as the culprit.

Dealing With Pollutants

By becoming more centered (see above), you are intuitively led to make proper choices. You can also go to your alpha level when undecided and ask. The first impression that comes is usually the strongest and the right one.

Ending Drug and Other Addictions

There are no simple answers to this problem. When a person opts for drugs, it is a mental decision based on his or her own past experiences. Several paths, described elsewhere, are applicable here:

1. The thirty-two-hour Silva Method training.
2. Subjective communication by another person toward changing his or her mind.
3. Clinical assistance (could be the result of option 2).

Session 37
Why Heal?

1. Close your eyes and roll them slightly upward toward your eyebrows.
2. Steps 2A, 3A, 3B, and 3C are optional. Count from 10 to 1.
   A. Starting with your scalp, focus your conscious awareness on the different parts of your body from head to toe, relaxing them as you go.
3. When you reach the count of 1, hold a picture of yourself in your mind as youthful, radiant, healthy, and attractive.
   A. Ask yourself mentally, "Why do I have this physical problem?" Then let your mind wander.
   B. When you find yourself thinking about a certain person, picture that person.
   C. Picture yourself forgiving each other. Imagine a hug or a handshake, smiles, and heads nodding in agreement. Feel good about this.
4. Repeat mentally, "I will always maintain a perfectly healthy body and mind."
5. Say to yourself, "I am going to count from 1 to 5; when I reach the count of 5, I will open my eyes, feeling fine and in perfect health, feeling better than before."
6. Count. When you reach 3, repeat, "When I reach the count of 5, I will open my eyes, feeling fine and in perfect health, feeling better than before."
7. At the count of 5, open your eyes and affirm mentally, "I am wide awake, feeling fine and in perfect health, feeling better than before. And this is so."

A medical doctor writes, "In an intuitive way, I believe from the time life begins one is aware of the true nature of healing, in the fact that it is not mechanical or remedy oriented. . . . A typical example is the so-called spontaneous remission of an incurable cancer. I would rather have this spontaneous event entitled creative or self-induced healing or hard work miracle."

So would I, doctor.

The author is Bernard S. Siegel, M.D., who, with his wife, Barbara H. Siegel, wrote "Spiritual Aspects of the Healing Arts" for *The American Theosophist.* Later Dr. Siegel wrote *Love, Medicine, and Miracles,** which was a long-time best-seller. A surgeon in private practice and assistant chemical professor of surgery at Yale University School of Medicine, Dr. Siegel in 1978 originated the "Exceptional Cancer Patient" group therapy, which works with patients' images and drawings. He does not believe that the physician should be merely a healing "mechanic." He sees the doctor also as a teacher helping people to take responsibility for their own problems and sharing in the healing work.

Again, I say, I agree, doctor. But we should go much further.

Why should it come as news that we make ourselves sick and well by mental means? Shouldn't this be as basic to our knowledge as the three Rs?

Yes, we need to teach our children how to use their minds to divide nine cookies among three children. But we also need to teach them how to go to an imaginary world and make corrections in the physical world—for instance, to get rid of a tummy ache from eating too many cookies.

Is It Wrong to Heal?

Sometimes people challenge this type of healing by calling it an invasion of privacy. Or they accuse Silva practitioners of inhibiting people from working out their own karma. Or they feel God does not want us to interfere.

My belief is that we are responsible for one another. If we

*New York: Harper & Row, 1986.

become aware that a person is suffering from a problem and that problem keeps the person from doing his or her job on this planet, it is our responsibility to correct that person's problem whether the person knows we are doing so or not.

As far as karma is concerned, I believe that karma refers to wrong things we do in this lifetime and the penalties they carry. Many Eastern philosophies teach that karma is carried over from one lifetime to the next. But I believe punishment to be valid only when we know, or are made aware of, what we did wrong. Its purpose should be to enable us to correct our ways and learn not to make the same mistake again. Punishment for a transgression we are unaware of has no effect or value. In the Silva Method, I attempt to show people the cause-and-effect relationship between their thinking and the results in their lives, so they can understand what they must change if they are to have perfect health, prosperity, and happiness.

With regard to interfering with God's will, I argue that if God did not want us to act, our actions and efforts would never be effective. But this is not the case. So the possibility that God doesn't want our interference does not relieve us of the obligation to *try* to correct problems.

We need to help one another. In kill-and-be-killed jungle life, animals come to the rescue of one another. We have first aid, ambulances, hospitals, nurses, paramedics, physicians, specialists, and healers of all types, including spiritual healers. My position is this: we have an obligation to develop our mental healing ability and to use it when necessary. I believe that we are on this planet for a purpose: to help with continued creation.

Humanity's Role in Creation

To help with creation, we need to be creators, not destroyers. We must strive to be part of the solution, not the problem. We must feel that creating is good and destroying, bad. If our mission were the destruction of the planet, this formula would be reversed. We would have a good feeling about knocking things down and blowing things up, and a bad feeling about building, inventing, and improving.

It is said we are created in God's image. Certainly our Creator does not have a body with two arms and two legs. So we are not made in the physical image of our Creator. It is the nonphysical image—the mental and spiritual image—that we reflect. To continue with creation, as the Creator's co-creators, we need to keep in touch with the boss. Workers on a building site who fail to touch base with their foreman and superiors are soon working at cross purposes.

The survival of humanity depends on our maintaining a connection with God—and not through our bodies but through our minds. We must learn to use the full potential of our God-given minds.

Mind is the sensing faculty of human intelligence. We know that human intelligence can function at a distance from the brain and that our awareness is not physically limited by the brain or the physical barriers of time and space.

When we turn our awareness away from the physical dimension and to the nonphysical, or spiritual, dimension, we come into touch with God. When we "turn off" the outside world—closing or defocusing our eyes, meditating, going to "the kingdom within"—we "turn on" our connection to God. We become Godly inspired. We become correct. We can guess right. We can even prophesy. We can heal. We can make this a better world to live in.

Session 38
Clairvoyance

1. Close your eyes and roll them slightly upward toward your eyebrows.
2. Steps 2A, 3A, 3B, and 3C are optional. Count from 10 to 1.
   A. Starting with your scalp, focus your conscious awareness on the different parts of your body from head to toe, relaxing them as you go.
3. When you reach the count of 1, hold a picture of yourself in your mind as youthful, radiant, healthy, and attractive.
   A. Ask yourself mentally, "Why do I have this physical problem?" Then let your mind wander.
   B. When you find yourself thinking about a certain person, picture that person.
   C. Picture yourself forgiving each other. Imagine a hug or a handshake, smiles, and heads nodding in agreement. Feel good about this.
4. Repeat mentally, "I will always maintain a perfectly healthy body and mind."
5. Say to yourself, "I am going to count from 1 to 5; when I reach the count of 5, I will open my eyes, feeling fine and in perfect health, feeling better than before."
6. Count. When you reach 3, repeat, "When I reach the count of 5, I will open my eyes, feeling fine and in perfect health, feeling better than before."
7. At the count of 5, open your eyes and affirm mentally, "I am wide awake, feeling fine and in perfect health, feeling better than before. And this is so."

Congratulations! Only two more days until you have completed the course.

What Makes You Clairvoyant?

You are in control of your alpha level. You are using it to help yourself and others. You decide to help your brother, who has gallstones. Although he lives a thousand miles away, you go to your alpha level, visualize him, and imagine the stones in his gallbladder. You sense two stones. You crush them with your fingers. You end your alpha session.

The next day he telephones.

"Just wanted you to know I passed the gallstone this morning. I'm finished with it."

"Maybe," you reply, "but I think there are two and you will pass another."

He telephones the next day. "You were absolutely right."

Can you imagine the exhilaration you feel! You have used your mind in a superhuman way! You can do it! Now you understand more about yourself.

What is going on? Are you clairvoyant? A dictionary definition of *clairvoyance* is "the supposed power to perceive things that are out of the natural range of human senses." But it is really not a sensory path that does the work. It is the mind that does the work.

First you get the desire to know something about your brother. Then you activate more of your mind. You get an idea about what you want to know. You express this idea in mental pictures, words, and feelings. You mentally picture the two gallstones. A clairaudient might mentally hear the answer. A clairsentient might mentally feel the information. But it is not the eyes, ears, or feelings that do the information gathering. It is the mind.

The mind includes all the senses. By all, I mean not only the standard five senses we are accustomed to singling out, but also many more sensory systems that we have not yet recognized, much less given names to. A clairvoyant can use all the subjective senses. As a clairvoyant, you have ESP, or extrasensory perception. In the Silva Method, we say ESP stands for effective sensory projection.

We feel that ESP is not extra. Everybody has it. Nor is it extrasensory, because it uses the senses. When sensing information from the subjective dimension, we do so through what is called general ESP, a combination of all the senses. It will make it more difficult for you to picture the problem or feel the problem if you focus on only one means of sensing.

Desire to know. Then information will come to you. You can make a mental picture of it, or put it into words or feelings—however you can focus in on it most easily and understand it most deeply. But the information comes first as a sense of knowing.

Does Having ESP Make You Strange?

Knowing how to go to your alpha level and use both hemispheres of your brain places you on the frontier of humanity's gradual development. This means that you are ahead of most people. Most people are simply lost in the crowd. When you are ahead of the majority, you are a stand-out. Many would prefer being nondescript over being a stand-out, because standing out carries with it the stigma of being strange. Many great geniuses were considered strange.

Actually, having ESP does not make you a stand-out. Everybody has it. You are one of billions. What makes you different now is that you know how to control and use it to solve problems. In that way you are a stand-out. If it makes you uncomfortable to be a stand-out, do not tell others what you are doing. Do not brag about how you got rid of a pain in seconds or quickly ended a respiratory problem. Keep these facts to yourself. If somebody asks you what you did, tell that person to read this book or to take the Silva training. Do not brag about helping somebody else to get rid of a health problem. Be satisfied to keep it to yourself, knowing that you have helped with creation.

Ego satisfaction is a superficial form of remuneration. You deserve better. And God rewards His co-creators in ways that are far superior to standard minimum wages. It was Kahlil Gibran, author of *The Prophet,* who reminded us that we should not invite a rich man to our house for dinner. He will merely invite us to his house for dinner in return. Invite a poor man to your house for dinner. This man will not be able to pay you back, so the universe will do so instead.

The universe "pays" in magnificent ways.

Session 39
Finding Your Purpose in Life

1. Close your eyes and roll them slightly upward toward your eyebrows.
2. Steps 2A, 3A, 3B, and 3C are optional. Count from 10 to 1.
   A. Starting with your scalp, focus your conscious awareness on the different parts of your body from head to toe, relaxing them as you go.
3. When you reach the count of 1, hold a picture of yourself in your mind as youthful, radiant, healthy, and attractive.
   A. Ask yourself mentally, "Why do I have this physical problem?" Then let your mind wander.
   B. When you find yourself thinking about a certain person, picture that person.
   C. Picture yourself forgiving each other. Imagine a hug or a handshake, smiles, and heads nodding in agreement. Feel good about this.
4. Repeat mentally, "I will always maintain a perfectly healthy body and mind."
5. Say to yourself, "I am going to count from 1 to 5; when I reach the count of 5, I will open my eyes, feeling fine and in perfect health, feeling better than before."
6. Count. When you reach 3, repeat, "When I reach the count of 5, I will open my eyes, feeling fine and in perfect health, feeling better than before."
7. At the count of 5, open your eyes and affirm mentally, "I am wide awake, feeling fine and in perfect health, feeling better than before. And this is so."

Congratulations! Only one more day until you have completed this course and can put all the resources of the Silva Method to work for you and your loved ones and friends.

Recognizing Your Purpose in Life

Is it healthier to be a drifter and have no goal or purpose for living or to have a purpose in life, to set goals, reach them, and go on to new ones?

Experience shows that drifters have less interest in life, less of a will to live, and are, therefore, more subject to despondency, unhappiness, and depression than purposeful people. They live to escape, usually via the bottle, until they attain the ultimate escape. The person who senses a purpose in life is more energetic, zestful, enthusiastic, and healthy. It does not matter what the purpose is, as long as it is faced with confidence and patience. It is wholesome to stop occasionally and remind yourself of your purpose in life.

When a person who is trained in the use of the right-brain hemisphere analyzes world events, he or she finds that humanity seems to have lost its sense of values in many areas. We are functioning as though we were sent to this planet on a vacation. We appear to be on a constant coffee break.

Some interesting and obvious answers come when a person uses the psychic level to consider such questions as: Where did we come from? Why are we here? What is our purpose? Then we perceive that we have been assigned by our Creator to this planet to take care of creation. When we analyze our strong natural program—to marry and to raise a family—we see that this is the system by which the Creator sees to it that more humans continue to enter the planet.

Likewise, the desires to be healthy and to avoid pain and discomfort ensure that we will be in good condition to do high-quality work. The desire to accumulate wealth is consistent with the purpose of correcting problems. What aspect of creation is your specialty? Are you currently on target? You can get answers to such questions at the alpha level:

1. Go to alpha level. Deepen your level.
2. Visualize yourself in front of you.

3. Ask yourself what your purpose is on this planet.
4. Permit yourself to daydream about it.
5. End your alpha session; continue to muse about the idea that came.

What you daydreamed about may be closer to what you should be doing than what you are doing.

When you are not doing what you should be doing, your job feels boring, unfulfilling, and unsatisfying—all stressful conditions that can affect your health. At the very least, this means you will not be as vibrant, energetic, and attractive to other people as you could be.

Session 40
Peace of Mind

This is the final morning of training. You know the procedure by now. Count from 10 to 1.

Congratulations! You have completed the course. From now on you are ready to use the Standard 5-to-1 method for reaching the alpha level.

You are now at that point when you are able to amaze the medical profession with your ability to snap back from any disease or injury with incredible speed and, of even more importance, to ward off illness and maintain a high level of healthful well-being.

The Kind of Person You Are

A United Press International story out of Los Angeles was headlined, "Grandma's visit sparks boy's fantastic recovery from tumor."

The nine-year-old youngster had been admitted to the hospital in critical condition. Doctors said he had a brain tumor and could die at any time. A foundation arranged for the grandmother to fly to Los Angeles. It was doubtful that the boy could live to her arrival, but he did. She arrived on a Friday. His improvement was instantaneous. On Sunday, he was taken off the critical list. A nursing supervisor stated that his tumor was in a state of remission.

This youngster probably had some personality trait that was demanding of love. Its arrival spelled remission.

In 1959, cardiologists Meyer Friedman and Ray Rosenman made the wire services when they disclosed that people were basically of two types, one more prone to heart attacks than the other. Type A people were impatient, competitive, ambitious, and prone to anger; Type Bs were more relaxed and easy-going. Of course, Type As were the more likely ones to become cardiac patients. Recently, these findings were distilled further, and the quality *hostility* stood out among those distinguishing Type As. In fact, *cynicism,* a distrust of human nature and contempt for people's motives, was found to be the key to the Type A personality.

The kind of person you are affects your health. Are you able to create on the Creator's "team"? Are you able to work harmoniously with your fellows? If the answer is no or maybe, then there is no "maybe" about your need to use your alpha level to program a more positive attitude toward others.

Here are some of the statements you can make to yourself that will change hostility and cynicism into trust and cooperation:

- I have greater and greater understanding, compassion, and patience with others.
- Every day I have more and more trust in myself and in others.
- I find it easier and easier to work with other people.

Hidden behind these words is another subliminal program. As you affirm these words at the alpha level, you are also saying, "Every day in every way I am getting healthier and healthier."

Healthier in every way, because it is not just the heart and circulatory system that reflect Type A and Type B characteristics. Here are some of the questions that were asked in a cancer and stress survey: Do you have a hobby? Do you tend to keep your feelings to yourself? In the last three years, have you experienced divorce or separation, a death in the family, financial difficulties, job difficulties? You already know the results of this survey. You know that the situations named can make us sick. The result need not be cancer. It can be a weakened immune system, which is an open invitation to just about any disease.

The apathetic person who says resignedly, "I am the way I am" can be giving himself or herself a death sentence. But, having finished this course, you now know how to change all that around.

Peace of Mind

Be willing to go to your alpha level and give yourself positive programming to change the way you are—and live longer.

A salamander whose tail has been bitten off can grow a new tail. Humans have not yet acquired the ability to grow a new organ or a new limb. We have a lot to learn about controlling our bodies. But one thing we are learning is that we can stop growing tumors and cultivating illnesses by eliminating our thoughts of conflict, resentment, and despair. If these thoughts won't go away by themselves, we can drive them away with thoughts of forgiveness and love. Then we will discover peace of mind. Every cell of your body will feel the difference once you make this discovery. It will seem as if the dark clouds have disappeared and the brilliant sun has once again begun to shine. The climate for healthy growth will have been restored.

Teilhard de Chardin wrote, "Someday, after we have mastered the winds, the waves, the tides, and gravity, we shall harness for God the energies of love. Then, for the second time in the history of the world man will have discovered fire." Doctors see diseases in the waiting room, not men, women, and children. How can they love a disease? In their jobs, these doctors are more like mechanics than lovers of people.

You and your family need to supply the love and forgiveness that nourish people's lives. You and your family need to supply the love, forgiveness, laughs, joys, music, hopes, and prayers that are so essential to the healing of the mind. Once you have supplied these, watch the healing miracle happen.

The Silva Method techniques to end stress, restore self-confidence and optimism, communicate forgiveness subjectively, and program positive thoughts and attributes are concrete steps you can take now to demonstrate such healing.

A Summary of the Implications of Healing

- It is right to heal; it is less right to ignore your role in your own healing and the healing of others.
- Healing is part of our role as co-creators with the Creator.
- We can reinforce our co-creatorship by going to alpha and activating the right brain.
- In the process, we improve our personalities, peace of mind, and health.
- Being able to detect problems at a distance is a natural, right-brain (psychic) function.
- The world is slowly beginning to realize the healing ability of the human mind.
- You have a purpose in life; sensing this purpose and going about its fulfillment will make life go more smoothly.

Part Two
The Silva Vision

Chapter 41
The World Tomorrow

Can you imagine how life on earth would be if everybody used both brain hemispheres? What would the effect be on world peace if differences between individuals—including world leaders—were addressed subjectively, Higher Self to Higher Self, and not as matters of *who* is right but of *what* is right? How would it be if geologists and other scientists were able to determine psychically the location of energy and mineral sources at will? What would bicameral business management be like, with executives able to make dependable key decisions intuitively? What would the health-care profession be like if doctors switched their emphasis from treating illness to keeping patients healthy, and used the power of their minds more than chemicals and medications to make them well?

I think it would be a better world. In fact, I think we would be on our way to creating a heaven on earth. The Orwellian prediction that in 1984 government would be in control seems to have been what indeed it was intended to be: fiction. There will be no Big Brother, but with all of us attuned to our intuition, there will be an even bigger Father.

The task of this chapter is to share with you my personal philosophy and my own intuitive concepts of the future.

The New Frontier: Inner Space

Physicist Rupert Sheldrake* has developed a concept to explain intuitive functioning. In this view, called "formative causation," there is a larger mind for each form of life, and each life form programs that larger mind. You and I, as we live and learn,

*Author of *The Presence of the Past* (New York: Time Books, 1988).

are feeding our learning into this larger mind. Dr. Sheldrake calls this mind, which is reminiscent of Dr. Carl Jung's collective unconscious, a morphogenetic field. Similarly, Peter Russell sees a global brain. He sees planet earth as able to regulate itself through a vast intelligence. Fritjof Capra sees the new physics as corroborating the wisdom of ancient Chinese philosophers, who saw the material world as having a spiritual basis.

Scientists are currently pioneering a new frontier: inner space. They are acknowledging the important role that consciousness plays in the physical realm. Not very long ago, scientists held a mechanistic view, a material philosophy. They rejected or ignored all the power of consciousness. Many scientists still hang on to this position, despite demonstrations of the effects of consciousness on matter. But scientists who have the courage to stand by their convictions are pioneering a brave new understanding of the world that holds existence to be more than an accidental result of a big bang.

We are beginning to see the world in a new light, the light of consciousness and intelligence. This could well be our ultimate enlightenment. What are some of the ways you can lead your life in a more enlightened way?

Before I share with you my views of where you and I are headed, let me remind you that we are still babes in the woods. We have achieved great things in the objective, physical dimension. We are veteran explorers of the earth, the sky, the sea, and even outer space. But in the subjective dimension, we are still infants. Even today's most proficient clairvoyants are only small children compared to those who will emerge. The abilities we will acquire as right-brain/left-brain humans will rival the dreams of science fiction.

Everybody Will Learn to Go to Alpha

With only 10 percent of the population now able to go within and use both hemispheres of the brain, we are relegated to the status quo. Explorations of our communal intelligence, what Rupert Sheldrake calls the morphogenetic field, suggests that a critical number must be involved in learning. Once that critical number is reached, then everybody "knows" or "is able."

We do not know what the critical number is for human beings, but we need to accelerate the training so that more and more of the 90 percent of humanity who are still innocent of their right-brain powers will learn to function intuitively, perceptively, creatively, and clairvoyantly. We must train all parents and parents-to-be, so that they can train their children. Once that happens, all people will be bicameral in their thinking. The religions and churches must get behind the concept to encourage right-brain usage. We have already lost two thousand years of practice by ignoring Christ's advice to enter the Kingdom of Heaven and become prophets and wise men so that everything would come to us.

Education must move faster in injecting right-brain activation into the learning process. By learning to function from the centers of their brain-frequency spectrum (alpha), students can become perfectly balanced in their thinking, using both brain hemispheres for easier, faster learning and the geniuslike ability to solve problems.

Music will then be combined with science and art with mathematics. Lesson outlines will come to reflect the two hemispheres' abilities. Memory courses will include visualization and imagination techniques. Speed reading and speed learning systems will become standard procedure, as will the use of biofeedback equipment, such as the Silva Educator. This instrument automatically turns on an educational program when the student reaches the desired level of relaxation and concentration—and turns off the program if the student leaves that level.

As more and more people acquire the ability to use both brain hemispheres, the morphogenetic field will become programmed for bicameral mental functioning, which will then become our way of life. No longer will we live in a left-brain world; instead, we will inhabit a left-brain/right-brain world. We will have completed another phase of evolution on this planet. We will all have the ability to recognize and alter disease-causing attitudes and emotions within ourself. We will all know how to recognize stress and use the alpha level to insulate ourselves against it. Should we take ill, we will know how to correct the problem mentally, and if a physician's services are needed, we will be able to support his or her therapeutic work, ensuring its success and accelerating the cure.

For bicameral physicians, diagnosis will be swifter and more accurate. Most expensive and often risky tests will be bypassed as human clairvoyance becomes activated to determine the nature of the problem. Doctors of the near future, because of their training in the use of the whole mind, will be skilled in the hypnosis and hypnoanalysis necessary to get to the mental cause of physical problems.

Clairvoyant psychiatrists will project into their patients' dreams or hallucinations to better understand their problems, whether psychological or biological in nature. These practitioners will be able to enter the patient's past whether the patient is present or not to find the roots of the problems.

Doctors and their patients will work together in the healing event. Doctors will explain the patients' physiological problems in a pictorial way so that patients can use visualization at the alpha level to cure themselves. As a result, healing will take place in a fraction of the time it takes now. The high cost of medical services will be reduced. The patient load at hospitals will be eased. As people become better able to ward off stress, they will stay healthier and life expectancy will rise.

We who operate vehicles will use our ability to transcend space and time with our intelligence. Therefore, we will be able to avoid accidents. As we activate our right brains, we will strengthen our intuition. People with a high intuitive factor consciously move, function, and act in a timely way to escape dangers. Strong survival programming expresses itself through both brain hemispheres and we will therefore intuitively stop smoking, taking drugs, and practicing other destructive habits. Our survival will be further ensured by our strengthened immune systems, our natural inclination to exercise physically, and our stronger attraction to the right food, air, water, and sleep.

Will we live forever? No. But we will all pass on without the debilitation, pain, and health problems of old age.

What Life Can Be Like

Besides our good health we will see other significant changes as we all learn how to go to alpha and use both brain hemispheres in controlled ways. Everyday business will be far from what we know it to be today. Executives will make use of their activated intuition and clairvoyance to reach accurate business decisions. There will be fewer, if any, business failures. The order of the day will be the right product in the right place at the right time, for decision makers and producers will be able to accurately assess the needs of the public.

Personnel directors will always hire the right people for the jobs. Production managers will be able to control quality through clairvoyance and subjective communication. Labor and management will be able to work together harmoniously for the common good. Financiers will use clairvoyance to make their investment decisions. Industrialists will know what to manufacture for future consumption that will preserve the environment while providing the greatest service to humanity. Graduating students will intuitively be drawn to the work they are best suited for and that best fits the needs of the time and place. Young people will listen less to the calls of glamor, glitter, and fame, and more to the calls of talent and productivity.

There will be no shortages of natural resources in the world, as we learn to live with what we have. And what we have will become more accessible as we learn to intuitively find what we need and recognize alternative resources. Petroleum engineers and geologists will use their minds to dowse for oil and minerals underground, detecting type, depth, quantity, and quality, and avoiding the expensive misses and dry holes now necessary.

Ranchers and farmers, responsible for providing food for human survival, will use clairvoyance to select the proper breeds and the best seeds. When they are centered in their thinking, their work will be more in tune with Mother Earth—they'll plant and reap the right crops at the right time in the right place, properly fertilized, transported, stored, and distributed. Law enforcement agencies will use their mental abilities to detect crime and apprehend criminals, and crime will decrease, owing to these enhancements. People with criminal tendencies will be identified in advance of perpetrating crimes and taught to function in a superior manner.

Government leaders will be more candid, open, and sincere. They will be able to mentally project into the future, both to the needs of their people and the actions of neighboring peoples. Differences will be detected while still small and solved with subjective communication. Wars between nations will ease as the element of surprise is eliminated and the crisis of distrust defused.

People will be more humane. There will be more respect for life in all forms. People will be quick to understand and quick to forgive, as exclusivity diminishes and unity is forged. There will be peace, health, and happiness on earth.

Is this reward enough for spending a few minutes on forty mornings to learn to use the alpha level for any purpose you desire?

The Road Back to the Father

Humanity has lost its way. Humanity has descended so deeply into the material, left-brain realm that our connection to the spiritual, right-brain realm has been left behind. Perhaps the first false step was taken in the Garden of Eden, when humanity first ate of the tree of the knowledge of good and evil. This is the material polarity on which the left brain thrives. Perhaps it continued in the days of the Tower of Babel, where many languages were spoken — meaning more left-brain specialization. The fact remains that, however we reached this pass, today we are a left-brain people, deaf to the voice of the Father within us.

When the greatest healer of all time, Jesus, was asked where he obtained certain information, his reply was, "From the Father." He had never lost his connection to the Father. Throughout the decades in which the Silva Method was developed, many "coincidences" involving Jesus occurred. During the early years, these helped to assure me I was on the right track. I discovered that people who activated their right hemispheres become more spiritual, more human. A human is not somebody who merely looks human. A human is somebody who also acts human. "By their fruits shall ye know them."

Alpha is the spiritual dimension. It is the source of intuition. Intuition is the voice of a Higher Intelligence than our own. It is the source of forgiveness, love, and trust, the attributes that Jesus taught. He exhorted us to live these qualities. But how can we do so when we permit our left brains to dominate our lives? The left brain thrives on separation, conflict, and ego.

Jesus exhorted us to seek the kingdom of heaven within us (the alpha) and to function within God's righteousness, taking care of God's creatures with forgiveness, love, and trust. If we did so, He promised, everything would fall in place. "And everything else will be added unto you." Especially good health. Because alpha is the connection to God.

Can you imagine what would have happened here on earth if we understood Jesus's message originally? We would be living in paradise now. We would be doing our thinking at ten cycles, and everybody would not only be closer to God but would be more Godlike.

But it is not too late. You have the key in your hand. Use it and everything else will be added unto you.

Five . . . four . . . three . . . two . . . one . . .

Part Three
Specific Applications

This section is meant as a quick reference guide for specific applications. In some instances, material presented in the text is repeated here for your convenience.

Chapter 42
Correcting Abnormal Behavior

Whenever you use subjective communication to normalize aberrant behavior, the recipient appears to have an immediate change of heart. An obstreperous neighbor behaves more neighborly. A dissident worker becomes more cooperative. A reluctant customer decides to buy. A rebelling family member reforms. A smoker seeks help to stop smoking.

When subjective communication is used to end destructive or life-threatening behavior in another person, it appears to take effect more readily and faster than when used in less critical matters. The brain neurons are programmed in many ways, but the one overriding priority is survival. The survival message you send objectively is readily accepted. Also, when you consider that at alpha you are activating your right hemisphere, which is your connection to your source, then you realize that your Higher Self is sending the message. The message goes from Higher Self to Higher Self. Can the brain neurons ignore a message from that direction?

You can achieve everything described above—and much more—by communicating subjectively. But do not think you will find the key here to gaining your way at home or in the office. Remember mutuality is a basic requirement. You cannot create a solution for yourself while creating a problem for somebody else. You can influence a person in the direction you choose only if that direction is the proper one to take.

Certainly it is a proper direction to take for a smoker to want to break the habit.

You already know how to program yourself to stop your smoking habit, and you know that these steps cannot be thrust on another person. That person has to make the personal decision to stop smoking and then be motivated to take each step in turn.

I have shown you how to use mental movies to break your own habits, but motivating others is made to order for subjective communication. The procedure is this:

1. Go to your alpha level.
2. Visualize the person.
3. Mentally speak to the person about the habit in a loving way. Point out how it would benefit the person, as well as that person's family and co-workers, including yourself, for him or her to end the habit (stop smoking).
4. End your alpha session.

Motivating a Person to Stop Smoking

The words you choose—Step 3—are the key to success. It would not be appropriate for me to give you these words. They must be your own words. You must have a sincere feeling for what you are saying. Your personal enthusiasm for what you are doing provides the "wattage" for your "broadcast."

However, let me stimulate your thinking by listing a number of mutual-benefit statements you might use in such a subjective conversation. You might say the following:

- "You will live longer if you stop smoking. We all love you and want you to live a long, healthy life."
- "Your breath will smell cleaner, a benefit to me. You will enjoy your food more as your sense of taste improves, a benefit to you."
- "You will save money. You will avoid burning the furniture. You and your family will be better off."
- "Your teeth and fingers will no longer be discolored. You will be more attractive to others."
- "As a nonsmoker, you will no longer be a slave to that package and you will be more accepted socially by others."

All of the above must be stated and felt in a loving way. But what if you dislike the person? What if the person is the bane of your existence? That noise you just heard on the line was a disconnect. Any kind of animosity, prejudice, resentment, rivalry, or other negative emotion is a separation. Separate yourself from the subject in any way and you break the connection.

You must clean the slate. This is called forgiveness. You already know that the procedure for forgiveness is to be mutually given and mutually received, subjectively. This step must be the first part of your imaginary conversation. It might go like this:

"I forgive you for all of our past misunderstanding and ask, in turn, to be forgiven by you."

Then see a handshake, a hug, or whatever symbol of a clean slate is appropriate in the relationship.

You should soon see the result of your subjective communication in the person's desire to break the habit. The person might talk about that desire to quit, or buy a book or a cassette tape on how to do it, or seek clinical help—or perhaps enroll in a Silva Method seminar.

Motivating the End of Any Habit

Any unwanted habit—alcoholism, overeating, gambling, nail biting, hair twiddling—can be attacked in this way. Have a subjective conversation to motivate the person to break it. Where there is a will to get rid of the habit, there will be a way.

J.A. had been in and out of prison from 1961 to 1981. During the last fifteen of those years he was a heroin addict.

"I have tried everything," he wrote, "from individual psychotherapy to group therapy, encounter groups, and back to individual counseling, both in and out of prison. None of these things helped me in the least. I gained more knowledge about myself, but the affliction remained."

J.A. then took the Silva Method training. A few weeks later he wrote,

It was not until this month that I saw any hope for recovery from my disease. Since the first weekend I have not felt the slightest urge to use heroin or anything else like addictive drugs in any form. You might say that this is too soon to praise the program, since

it has been only a few weeks. However, when you have lived in the shadow of your own self-destruction for fifteen years as I have, and have gone through all the horror and pain that I put myself through, you don't need to wait a year or two to know when something works. I am going to make it my business to tell any addict or other person, who wants help and will listen, about the Silva training. I know it is what I need to save my life, and I know it can save others like me.

Drug addiction has no simple answers. Still, there is one truth that has no exceptions: change your mind and you change your reality. J.A. changed his mind about himself while taking the Silva training. So his reality changed.

But, you say, an addiction creates a physical dependency. What about the physical symptoms of withdrawal? Change your mind and you change your body chemistry. This we know. This is the easiest point of all to understand. However, each person's reality goes beyond the body to the bodies of other people, to the minds of those people, to the immediate environment, the community, the country, the world, the universe, the Source. The seeds of excessive behavior can take root anywhere along the way. Little wonder that there is no pat answer to heroin addiction or addiction to some other substances—except a change of mind.

The Silva training can lead to that change of mind, as it did for J.A. So can subjective communication from a sincere person to the addict.

The aim of such communication should be to effect a change of mind and motivate the person to seek help, and the form of the conversation should conscientiously adhere to the fundamental requirements for successful right-brain communication. Needless to say, lesser habits not involving addictive substances that are nevertheless pesky, antisocial, unwanted habits will also respond to these basic steps: go to the alpha level and hold an imaginary conversation with the person, and encourage that person to change his or her mind, thereby motivating the person to do what needs to be done to modify the unwanted behavior.

Chapter 43
Insomnia, Headaches, and Weariness

If you are plagued with tension headaches, you can take over-the-counter pain relievers quite effectively. Millions of people do. But many of those who take aspirin regularly become plagued with another problem. This time it is in their stomachs. Aspirin can cause tiny holes in the stomach lining. These, in turn, can become ulcerous. Other aspirinlike pills can cause liver problems.

If you are depressed, you can take uppers. If you are nervous, you can take downers. If you cannot sleep, there are pills for that, too. It has been estimated that there are more than twenty-five million insomniacs in the United States and that well over $100 million is spent on prescription sleeping pills. Yet at a sleep disorder symposium held in New York City back in 1976, doctors reported that most of these prescriptions were a waste of money and that many such medications actually *caused* rather than cured insomnia.

Doctors at the Sleep Disorder Clinic at Stanford University reported that about 40 percent of the patients who complained of insomnia were actually losing sleep because they had become dependent on the drugs they were taking to treat the insomnia. After being taken off the drugs gradually, these patients slept on the average of 20 percent more, and many had no more sleep problems at all.

A subjective approach to problems that are subjectively caused is more direct and has no side effects. In the case of insomnia, first program yourself at alpha that whenever you go to alpha and count backward slowly, you will move in the direction of normal, natural sleep. Then, whenever you are lying awake unable to sleep, go to alpha. Begin counting backward from 200.

You may not get very far, as you slow your brain waves to theta and then delta—deep sleep.

To review, here is the basic formula to get rid of pesky attitudes and conditions:

1. Go to your alpha level.
2. Identify the problem.
3. Affirm its opposite—the solution.
4. Imagine the solution taking place.
5. End your alpha session.

Let us take some examples.

Starting with the problem of tension headaches, you would use this five-step procedure:

1. Count yourself into alpha in your usual way; it might be helpful to deepen your level with additional countdown exercises or with the progressive relaxation procedure.
2. Identify the problem, mentally saying, "I have a headache; I don't want to have a headache."
3. Affirm the solution, mentally saying, "When I end my session and open my eyes at the count of 5, I will no longer have a headache; I will feel fine."
4. Visualize yourself as if you were looking at yourself in a full-length mirror. You have a headache; you look like you have a headache. Move the picture slightly to the left—the headache is going away. Move the picture again to the left; imagine yourself free of the headache.
5. Count to 5, reminding yourself at the count of 3 that when you open your eyes at the count of 5, you will no longer have a headache, you will feel fine. When you reach 5, remind yourself again and open your eyes. If there is any remnant of the headache left, wait five minutes and repeat the process. Sometimes, in the case of severe migraine headaches, you may need three sessions, five minutes apart, to get relief.

Another example might be weariness. Apply the same basic formula:

1. Go to alpha in your usual way, and deepen your level.
2. Identify the problem by mentally verbalizing it: "I am tired and weary; I don't want to be tired and weary; I want to be full of energy, wide awake, rarin' to go."
3. Affirm the solution, mentally saying, "When I open my eyes at the count of 5, I will no longer be weary. I will be full of energy."
4. Visualize yourself weary. Move the picture to the left and imagine yourself perking up. Move the picture again to the left and imagine yourself dynamic and active.
5. Count to 5, reminding yourself before you count, at the count of 3, and when you reach 5, "I am wide awake, full of energy, feeling great."

Another time to apply this formula is when you feel down in the dumps. Here are the five steps applied in this unwanted condition:

1. Go to alpha. Deepen it.
2. "I feel down in the dumps, depressed. I don't want to feel down in the dumps or depressed. I want to feel enthusiastic, energetic, and optimistic."
3. "When I open my eyes at the count of 5, I will no longer feel down in the dumps. I will feel on top of the world."
4. Visualize yourself as you are. Move the picture to the left slightly and imagine yourself more "alive." Move the picture again slightly to the left and imagine yourself head up, shoulders back, animated, and eager.
5. "When I open my eyes at the count of 5, I'll feel great." Repeat at the count of 3 and again at 5, opening your eyes.

Chapter 44
Severe Chronic Depression

Depression is a serious problem that can lead to acute withdrawal, even suicide. The deeper the depression, the deeper are the levels of alpha needed to end it. Also, the more positive are the programming techniques that must be used and the more frequently they must be applied. Furthermore, with depression you need to use objective as well as subjective approaches.

Here are some steps in both categories that can be helpful.

Objective Approaches

1. See your physician, who might prescribe dietary supplements and medical steps.
2. Increase your physical activity. Exercise. Take long walks.
3. Be creative in your work. As you move from here to there in your work, you may have insights into the reasons for your depression.

Subjective Approaches

1. Go to alpha and meditate about your depression. Discover a reason for it.
2. Do the basic five-step exercise described in Chapter 43. Substitute "depression" in the formula. Do this three times a day.
3. Before falling asleep at night, go to alpha, put your thumb and first two fingers of either hand together, and tell yourself, "I will be in good spirits all day tomorrow."
4. When you feel physically depleted, it is good to give of yourself. This may seem contradictory, but things in the subjective realm are frequently reversed from the way

they are in the objective realm. In the subjective realm, the more you give, the more you have. When you help others, you also help yourself.

For depression, get involved in projects with other people, even if it means volunteering without monetary reward. When you are busy with constructive, creative activities that help to make this a better world to live in, your world gets rosier, too.

Chapter 45
Back Problems

Doctors are often frustrated with back problems that refuse to respond. Here is a representative example, from Barbara G. Parker, of Oklahoma City:

The last of August of 1983 I went to see a chiropractor because I had tried everything else. In two years nothing had helped. The medical doctors had put me to bed or on crutches and drugs, and still I had the same problems: right hip pains, right shoulder pain, headaches, neck pain, and insomnia. The chiropractor took X-rays in August and found deterioration of discs, loss of cervical curve, rotational misalignment of the cervical vertebrae, and curvature of the thoracic spine. Or, in plain words, the discs in my lower spine were closing and causing pressure on the nerves and making my leg hurt. After two months of therapy, the chiropractor suggested that I attend the Silva Method training. He had attended a few years ago. He hoped that it would help me.

Well, was he ever right! Our lecturer had some really good suggestions on how to imagine a healthy back. I went to level and programmed three times a day and started getting better. I took Silva in November. In January, X-rays showed that the disc that was closing was now open as it should be. I am sleeping all night and the problem is better. . . .

What visualization and imagination might Barbara Parker have used in helping her doctor to help her? The general answer: mentally picturing the body perfect. The specific answer: imagining the problem back discs separating.

I am reminded of the Alexander Technique, invented by the Australian actor F. Matthias Alexander in 1894. Suffering the loss of his voice during performances, he discovered that when he mentally and physically realigned his head and neck, his voice returned. Later, he found that by concentrating both mentally and physically on this postural change in others he was able to relieve many illnesses. The Alexander Technique is now taught on several continents. The mental component involves picturing the neck free and the head going upward to permit the back to lengthen and widen. When one holds that image in the mind and verbalizes the appropriate words, the body follows suit.

Other approaches have used mental imagery to help the body, but the Silva Method was the first to associate this imagery with the alpha level. This innovation enabled practitioners to activate more of their minds, enhancing the results of other visualization methods many times while increasing the applications of those methods widely.

If you have a back problem, go to your alpha level and imagine it being corrected. Use whatever you know about the problem in imagining that correction taking place. If your doctor says the discs are pressing together, as in Barbara Parker's case, imagine the discs of the spine moving apart. In fact, imagine that *you* are moving them apart.

Visualize yourself as if you were looking at yourself in a full-length mirror. In a second mirror to your left, imagine reaching inside yourself and stretching your spinal column. In your imagination, fix yourself up in any way that will leave your spine perfect.

Health care specialists need to imagine things with physiological correctness. They know what the discs of a spine look like, so they must use what they know. But you are not a doctor. You need not imagine things with physiological precision. You are identifying the problem to your brain neurons as you understand it. That is all your brain neurons require in order to know what you are referring to.

Similarly, a health-care specialist might have to perform a correction in the imagination much as it would be done on an operating table. But all you need to do is imagine the correction you need—in any way you can picture it. Your brain neurons will get the message.

If you need help in imagining what the spine looks like, look it up in your encyclopedia. This is a good idea, by the way, for any part of the body on which you are working. But do not demand a perfect picture of yourself. Mental pictures are our way of holding mental concepts, and it is really the *concept* of a spine that does the work. Mental pictures, therefore, do not have to be sharp and in wide-screen Technicolor. Accept your visualization. Some people will have more precise images than others, but all people, regardless of how they visualize and imagine, can help the healing process. The only requirement is that you do this thinking at alpha.

So, to fix a back problem, follow these steps:

1. Go to your alpha level.
2. Visualize yourself in front of you. You can sense through your body to the spine and visualize the back problem.
3. Imagine yourself fixing the back problem, separating the discs, straightening the vertebrae—doing whatever is necessary.
4. Move the picture slightly to the left and imagine the cure starting to take effect.
5. Move the picture again, slightly to the left; imagine yourself perfect.
6. End your session.

Chapter 46
Kidney Stones or Gallstones

If you have a stone in your kidney, how do you visualize it? It does not matter. Visualize the affected kidney. Imagine what a kidney stone might look like. Get rid of it. End your session.

But how, specifically, might you get rid of a stone? You can pulverize it with your fingers and imagine the powder dissolving in the urine. You can use a laser beam and imagine the tiny beam of light disintegrating the stone. Or, if you are to receive an ultrasound treatment, imagine the high-pitched sound disintegrating the stone and its powdered remnant dissolving in the urine and being passed painlessly from the body.

Here is the step-by-step procedure:

1. Go to your alpha level.
2. Visualize yourself in front of you. Visualize the stones in whatever part of the body they are; crush them with your fingers in your imagination.
3. Move the picture slightly to the left and complete the imaginary pulverizing of the stones; imagine them dissolving in the gland or the organ secretions and leaving the body.
4. Move the picture once more to the left and imagine no sign of stones; you are perfect.
5. End your session. Repeat morning, noon, and night.

The basic procedure is always the same. You go to your level. You identify the problem by visualizing it. You imagine fixing yourself up, moving the picture to the left. You imagine yourself again to the left, free of the problem. You end your session.

These are some options:

- You can go to alpha by counting down or by defocusing your eyes.
- You can deepen your alpha level with further countdowns or progressive relaxation.
- You can question the cause of your illness and, if another person is involved, go through a forgiveness procedure subjectively.
- You can imagine you are going on a trip inside your body or visualize yourself in front of you.
- You can add verbal affirmations mentally that you are becoming "better and better."

These options are up to you, depending on how you feel and the time you have available. Refer to previous chapters for the how-to steps involved.

Speaking of time, the optimum amount of time to spend on each session is fifteen minutes, with the bulk of that time devoted to fixing up the problem and imagining the arrival of the solution.

Chapter 47
Illnesses With Unknown Causes

How do you "fix" a problem that is so complicated or so poorly understood that visualization is difficult or impossible?

A.J. was a quadriplegic for eighteen years. He had total paralysis on one side, 8 percent paralysis on the other. The doctors told him that he had multiple sclerosis (MS), an incurable progressive disease, and that he would die in a few years. He decided to enroll in the Silva Method Training. The very first day of training to go to alpha, he noticed feeling return to one finger. Part way through the course he felt the urge to stop medication. By the end of the course, full use of his left arm had been restored.

A.J. began programming at the alpha level to reach specific goals. He wanted to be able to get out of the wheelchair and into a vehicle and drive that vehicle. Twice daily he went to his alpha level for a few minutes and created a mental moving picture of himself driving a vehicle. Within eight months he had attained the goal: he had acquired a van with a mechanism to raise his wheelchair from the sidewalk so he could swing himself into the driver's seat.

He set another goal of being able to walk and to climb stairs. Again he made mental movies, imagining himself walking up the stairway to enter a local sports arena. Fourteen months after taking the Silva Method training, he walked up those very stairs.

Many others who have had MS have helped themselves at alpha to reverse the disease or at least stop its progression. But they have not necessarily used mental pictures of the physiological problem involved. Very little is known about this condition, and even that which is known is too difficult for the average lay person to understand and visualize. It is easy to visualize spots on lungs, to erase those spots, to imagine healthy lungs, and thus to rid oneself of a cough. And it is easy to visualize light spots or islands on the pancreas, to imagine the removal of those spots, and to help normalize hypoglycemia. It is easy to visualize an injury to the stomach lining, then to visualize repairing it, and thus to end an ulcer problem. But there are many ailments, like MS, where visualizing the problem is not that easy. The procedure, then, is to do what A.J. did—imagine the *goal.*

In general, the goal is to get back to normal life, free of the inhibiting aspects of the problem. So, instead of imagining yourself fixing up the affected body area, imagine yourself getting out of bed, looking and feeling great, and going back to enjoying life.

Except for this change, the procedure is the same.

Chapter 48
Blood Vessel Problems

In the case of a problem involving a blood vessel to the heart, the procedure is as follows:

1. Go to your alpha level.
2. Visualize yourself in front of you with the heart problem—perhaps you have just walked up the stairs and the chest pains have started. Mentally picture yourself at the top of the stairs, hand to your chest. Do this for one or two minutes.
3. Move the picture slightly to the left (about fifteen degrees from straight ahead to sideways) and imagine a correction taking place; since the correction entails the removal of a coating called plaque that has accumulated on the walls of the veins or arteries, imagine the plaque dissolving. Imagine a change in blood chemistry that is doing the job or perhaps see an imaginary pipe cleaner or a laser beam doing the work. However you wish to imagine the improvement taking place is fine. Take twelve minutes to fix yourself up.
4. Again, move the picture slightly to the left (about fifteen degrees) and imagine your circulation system working perfectly and yourself without chest pains. You climb stairs, you run, you engage in all your activities. You are pain free. Spend one or two minutes with this picture.
5. End your session.

Note that I used *visualize* in Step 2, but *imagine* for Steps 3 and 4. Since we are not doctors, the correction step is not something we have seen before. So we imagine.

Chapter 49
Identifying Allergies

Your mind knows what is causing that skin irritation. Your mind knows why your sinuses get clogged. Your mind knows why you develop that cough. But your mind is not telling. You can get your mind to divulge the cause of your allergy. Here are several suggested approaches.

Let us assume three situations:

A. The cause is one of several possible known substances.
B. The cause is an unknown substance.
C. The cause is either a substance or something else.

A. When the cause of the allergy is one of several known foods or substances, because the time and place that the allergy occurs makes this self-evident, then here is the suggested procedure:

1. Go to your alpha level.
2. Visualize your physician in front of you. Or, if you prefer, visualize a prominent chemist or other scientist you respect.
3. Ask your authority whether the allergy is more likely to be caused by the first food or substance (name it) or the second food or substance (name it).
4. Move your attention away from the authority and on to the two foods or substances. An answer will come. Accept it.
5. Compare the substance now in question with the third food or substance, again asking the authority, disconnecting, and getting an answer to pop into your mind.
6. When you have compared all the foods or substances, one will have emerged as the culprit in this multiple-choice process.
7. End your alpha session.

B. We eat on the average about 1,400 pounds of food a year. This food contains about ten pounds of chemical additives, numbering several thousand preservatives; flavoring and coloring agents; stabilizers; and pesticides. Any one of these chemicals could conceivably cause an allergic reaction. It is better to identify and eliminate the irritant, or the food that contains it, than to program away the allergy symptoms, which might then reappear in some even less acceptable way.

When you do not know what foods or substances could possibly be involved, here is the suggested procedure:

1. Go to your alpha level.
2. Visualize your physician in front of you, or, if you prefer, a prominent chemist or other authority.
3. Ask your authority what food or substance is causing your allergy.
4. Disconnect—that is, start trying to figure out the cause of your allergy.
5. An answer will come. Accept it. Other impressions may come, but the first impression is usually the strongest—and the right one.

C. It is possible that the allergen is not a food or substance. For instance, for years, every time V.M. entered a room where there were roses, his eyes teared, his nose ran, and his sinuses got all stuffed up. Finally, he went to a doctor. The doctor said, "You have rose fever—an allergy to roses."

"But, doctor," replied V.M., "it even happens when I walk into a room with plastic roses."

The doctor paused. "It's emotional," he stated.

Later, V.M. took the Silva training. He decided to use his alpha level to go back in time to find if any event in his life connected to roses could have resulted in the allergy. He imagined himself beside a calendar and asked to know when the problem with roses started. He turned the pages of the calendar back, month after month, year after year. When he reached February of the year he was four years old, a scene began to unfold.

His mother answered the doorbell. A delivery man handed her roses—a Valentine's Day gift. She put them in her best vase, placed them on the piano, and disappeared back in the kitchen. V.M. had never seen roses before. He pulled over a stool, got up, and began to touch and smell the beautiful blossoms. All of a sudden, down they went. Crash! His mother came into the room, saw what happened, and began to scream at him.

V.M. now felt, at his alpha level, what he felt then. Panic.

His mother did not love him anymore. Who would take care of him? Feed him? Clothe him? He cried. All during the time his mother cleaned up the mess and put the roses in another vase, his tears flowed. Finally, she came over to him.

"Don't ever do that again." She patted him on the head and kissed him. He stopped crying and the scene ended.

Back at beta, V.M. realized what had happened. At age four, his mother had been his life-support system. When his mother stopped loving him, his life was threatened. The whole experience of "roses" was stored in the survival department of his brain. So whenever he came into the presence of roses, even years later, the alarm went off and the brain neurons in the survival department got busy. Perhaps the ensuing communications went something like this:

"Life threatened—roses."

"What did we do before?"

"We cried—and it saved our life."

"Let's do it again."

So the message went out to the eyes, the nose, and the rest of the crying mechanism. Each "life-saving" instance reinforced the "allergy" symptoms as a survival mechanism.

V.M. decided to go to a florist and observe the process. Armed with this new insight, he approached the roses in the refrigerated glass case, opened the sliding glass panel, sniffed their fragrance, and awaited the outpouring from his eyes and nose. It never came. V.M. later realized why. In identifying what had happened and shaking his head in amazement, he had thought, "How ridiculous. My mother never stopped loving me. My life was never threatened. Anybody would act that way if it happened to their roses." That new understanding had made a correction in the unwanted programming. Perhaps the neurons talked it over like this:

"Hey, fellows, roses have been misfiled. They should not be in our survival department."

End of allergy.

Chapter 50
Picking a Mate

Man-woman relationships improve immensely when both parties are able to use both hemispheres in a balanced way. Two centered wheels travel more smoothly than two eccentric wheels. People should acquire this centeredness before they choose a mate. It is said that people are generally only 20 percent accurate in choosing a mate. This is why there are so many divorces. Clairvoyants, on the other hand, average 80 percent accuracy.

Living together is not the answer. The decision to do so is usually based on the body alone, not the brain. Some people keep changing partners until, if they're lucky, they find the right one. Most animals have a better system than that. If just one person in a potential couple has taken the Silva Method or completed the instructions in this book, the chances for accuracy are improved, because that person can use the alpha level to evaluate the choice. Here are the steps:

1. Go to your alpha level and deepen it.
2. Put the thumb and first two fingers of either hand together.
3. Mentally picture yourself with your proposed mate and a calendar that reads the present year. Picture a wedding in progress.
4. Move the mental picture slightly to the left. Change the calendar to three years into the future. Observe how you appear toward each other.
5. Finally, move the picture slightly to the left, change the calendar to ten years into the future, and again observe your relationship.

You now have the "evidence" you need to make a decision in favor of or against the marriage.

When you are married, use of the alpha level has only begun.

Chapter 51
Successful Parenting

Every couple wants to have a healthy, normal child. The Silva Method is centered and in tune with the universal flow; free of excessive behavior, polluting habits, and negative thoughts; and oriented toward creativity. Such a pairing practically guarantees a healthy, normal child.

But the Silva-trained partners can go even further. They can program for a child destined for success. When the two partners decide that they want to have a child, they should enter the alpha level separately, each seeking to learn what the needs of the planet will be. Once they agree that the need is for a doctor, a scientist, or specialist in some particular field, they should go to alpha together and ask the Creator (Higher Intelligence, God) to send the correct intelligence through them, an intelligence that will contribute toward solving the planet's problems in the future.

The procedure is as follows:

1. Husband and wife go to deep alpha at separate times.
2. Imagine the planet directly ahead and ask, "What will be the planet's most important need in the future?"
3. Move the picture slightly to the left. Visualize a calendar with the year plainly in view—twenty years in the future. Remember what appears on the planet or comes to mind.
4. Again ask that question and move the picture slightly to the left with the year clearly in view thirty years in the future. Again, remember what appears or comes to mind.
5. End the alpha session.

If, after several attempts, the prospective parents cannot reach agreement on the skill priority, each should do a multiple-choice alpha session separately, using the skills that surfaced in order to determine an optimum choice. Once this has been determined, both partners go to level to ask for such a child. The asking procedure is simple:

1. Go to your alpha level together; deepen your alpha levels.
2. Each say aloud, "I'm ready."
3. Each ask mentally, "Higher Intelligence, send through us the correct intelligence who will help solve the planet's problem [insert determined need] in the future if that is your will. Amen."
4. Each should end the session in his or her own time.

Chapter 52
Starting a Child's Education Before Birth

After conceiving, the clairvoyant mother starts selecting lessons to read to the fetus. She will choose subject matter relating to the science or profession in which the newcomer will participate as an adult.

The clairvoyant mother will program the fetus to subconsciously record all the information she will provide. She will then read the selected material aloud. Later in life, the child will automatically become aware of this information.

This programming procedure is as follows:

1. After the fetus has been developing for one month or more, the mother goes to the alpha level and programs herself to awaken at the best time to program the fetus.
2. On awakening that night, the mother again goes to the alpha level and imagines the fetus in a mental picture straight ahead. She states mentally, "You will remember later, when you need to, what I tell you now." She pictures herself reading aloud to the fetus.
3. She moves the picture slightly to the left. The fetus is now larger and the head is bigger; she imagines a storehouse of information there.
4. She moves the picture again slightly to the left; the child has been born and is now an adult; the child knows all that has been read to it in the womb.
5. The mother goes to sleep from her alpha level.

The mother may now read information to the unborn child anytime it is convenient to do so. The mother can continue to teach her child after birth and before school starts. The child's best teacher and programmer is always the child's mother. The female, by nature being more subjective and intuitive, is able to communicate at this level to the child. At this level, learning takes place at any age faster and easier than at beta.

It is to be hoped that schools will recognize this early training when it becomes standard practice and will provide youngsters with an accelerated and specialized curriculum. It is entirely possible that children so programmed will earn a doctoral degree by age fifteen.

For those who disapprove of early learning, because we see some students finishing college who still do not know what they want as a career, there is the assurance that the intuitive mother will already *know* that child's future career choice.

A child who has been programmed before conception will enjoy exposure to the material the parents have chosen, and will understand it later in life more easily than other subjects. And a child who receives a doctoral degree at age fifteen will still be young enough to learn anything else if he or she so desires.

Chapter 53
Affecting the Weather

Lifting mental "fog" subjectively should be easier than lifting physical fog objectively, but even the latter is possible. Here is how Lucille V. King, Silva lecturer in Idaho, did it:

This recent winter weather with its snow and fog here in Northern Idaho brought back a memory of a morning in 1970 when John, my husband, and I had planned a trip to Dallas, Texas.

Coeur d'Alene is thirty-two miles from Spokane International Airport, which was recently called the foggiest airport in the world.

It was late February when we found our way very carefully over I-90 and reached the airport safely, only to find the airport fogged in.

They did allow us to board the plane, and we slowly taxied out to the end of the runway where we waited and waited for a break.

I was new at using our Silva Method techniques in those days, but decided to use the boredom of waiting to put the Silva Method to the test.

I said to John, "I am going to level to ask for help." This I did. I spoke to the fog and said, "Lift!" Moments later the captain came over the intercom with the words, "The fog has lifted and we are taking off." Above the clouds a moment or so later the pilot reported, "Spokane Airport fogged in again."

The coauthor of this book, Dr. Robert B. Stone, was showing some friends the sights on Kauai. "When we reached the top of Kokee, where there is an incredible view down to the valley of Kalalau," he relates, "it was all socked in by a pea soup fog. I told my friends to have some coffee in the refreshment shop and to rejoin me when they finished. I then went to the alpha level and visualized my energy of consciousness heating up the fog and melting it. When my friends emerged in ten minutes, the fog was gone and they gasped at the magnificent view."

We create our world. You can go to alpha and lift the fog.

Index